NEW YORK REVIEW BOOKS
CLASSICS

A BOOK OF
MEDITERRANEAN FOOD

ELIZABETH DAVID (1913–1992) was brought up in an
outwardly idyllic seventeenth-century Sussex farmhouse,
Wootton Manor, and her interest in cooking may well have
been a response to the less-than-stellar meals on offer there.
During World War II she lived in France, Italy, Greece, and
Egypt (where she worked for the Ministry of Information),
and spent much of her time researching and cooking local
fare. On her return to London in 1946 she began to write
cooking articles, and in 1949 the publisher John Lehmann
offered her a hundred-pound advance for *A Book of Mediterranean Food*. When it came out the following year, it
proved a revelation to Anglo-Saxon appetites. David's other
books include *Italian Food* (1951) and *Summer Cooking*
(1955; also published by NYRB Classics). She continued to
be a student of her art throughout her life. Always an
innovative force, she even persuaded Le Creuset to extend its
range of cookware colors by pointing at a pack of Gauloises.
"That's the blue I want," she said. Elizabeth David was
awarded a CBE, made a Chevalier de l'Ordre de Mérite
Agricole, and—the honor that pleased her most—elected a
Fellow of the Royal Society of Literature.

CLARISSA DICKSON WRIGHT is best known as half of TV's
Two Fat Ladies duo and cowrote that series' cookbooks. Her
other books include *The Haggis: A Little History* (1996) and
Food: What We Eat and How We Eat (1999).

ELIZABETH DAVID
A Book of Mediterranean Food

SECOND REVISED EDITION

DECORATED BY JOHN MINTON

NEW YORK REVIEW BOOKS

New York

This is a New York Review Book
Published by The New York Review of Books
435 Hudson Street, New York, NY 10014
www.nyrb.com

First published by John Lehmann 1950. This edition revised for Macdonald
and Co. by Elizabeth David and published in 1958. First revised
edition published by Penguin Books in 1955. Second revised edition 1965.

Library of Congress Cataloging-in-Publication Data

David, Elizabeth, 1913–
  A book of Mediterranean food / by Elizabeth David ; introduction by
Clarissa Dickson Wright.
     p. cm. — (New York Review Books classics)
  ISBN 1-59017-003-2 (pbk. : alk. paper)
  1. Cookery, Mediterranean. I. Title. II. Series.
  TX725 .D36 2002
  641.59'11822—dc21

                                    2002000749

ISBN 978-1-59017-003-8

Printed in the United States of America on acid-free paper.

10 9 8 7 6

TO

Veronica Nicholson

*

Contents

* *

Foreword

* * * * * * * * * * * * * * * * * * * *

I WAS three years old in 1950 when Elizabeth David's *A Book of Mediterranean Food* was published. Still, I have a very early memory of sitting on the floor by the bookshelves in my mother's study and looking at the pictures that John Minton had so lovingly crafted. I had never seen the blue of the Mediterranean, but I have carried it from that book's cover in my mind's eye ever since. The fact that when I did see it it wasn't like that at all is of no matter.

It is this vision of a land that existed solely in Elizabeth David's imagination which has shaped our food, our dreams, and our thinking over the past fifty years. Those who rush to buy holiday homes in France or Chiantishire (as Tuscany has now been renamed) or those endless books that have only to mention purple lavender fields or baskets of lemons to make the best-seller lists, all are searching for a place that isn't there except in the heart of this great food writer.

To Elizabeth David, the Mediterranean was about far more than food—it was her escape both mentally and physically from the restrictions of an English upper-class family in the chilly confines of Wootton Manor in Sussex. Born on Boxing Day, 1913, she came of good stock: her father's family found their fortune in Wales in the mid-1800s and her mother was the daughter of a viscount, the granddaughter of a lord, and the niece of a countess. Later, Elizabeth was related by marriage to the cream of society —the Cecils, the Shrewsburys, and the Palmers—and the arrogance and self-confidence of her background comes out in all her writing.

She was autocratic; she didn't suffer fools gladly and had all the precision of her age and class. You would never dare to speak to her of note paper if you meant writing paper, and this translated itself to the accuracy of her writing. Listen to this passage from *A Book of Mediterranean Food* and you will hear all the dismissiveness of the Edwardian high-born:

> The meat of young kid is much appreciated all over the Mediterranean, especially in the more primitive parts such as Corsica and the Greek islands. It is hard to say why there is such a prejudice against this animal in England, and it is only the gastronomically ignorant who, the moment they go abroad, suppose that whatever meat they are eating is disguised horse or goat. The textures of these meats are quite unlike those of veal, beef, or mutton, and there is besides no call for a French or Italian cook to pretend that he is serving mutton when it is in fact goat.
>
> In the same way, foreigners in the Middle East are often heard to complain that they are being served with camel instead of beef. If they had ever eaten camel meat they would soon know the difference.

A Book of Mediterranean Food was an act of courage on the part of its first publisher, John Lehmann. Postwar Britain was a gray, unhappy place, the scars of bomb sites a horrifying reminder of the recent hostilities. British food was probably at its lowest ebb ever, and the taste of Spam, dried egg, and Woolton Pie had soured the palates of its people. (This last, named after the Minister of Food, Lord Woolton, was a vegetable pie thickened with oatmeal and flavored with Marmite.) Most food was still rationed, and, except in the sinister streets of Soho, olive oil could only be bought in bottles marked "For External Use Only" in chemists' shops.

How dramatic a risk Elizabeth's first book was is evident from its very first recipe. Soupe au Pistou calls for French beans, tomatoes, vermicelli, garlic, sweet basil, Gruyère cheese, and potatoes. Most of these ingredients were entirely unavailable at the time. Indeed, only the last would have been at all easy to purchase.

Several things stand out about Elizabeth David: her perfectionism, her immaculate use of English, and her exquisite prose. An avid and eclectic reader, she scattered her work liberally with quotations from Arnold Bennett (an after-hours lunch at the finest restaurant in the world), Robert Byron (an octopus- and snail-filled Greek feast), Tobias Smollett (on the abundance of fish in Nice), D. H. Lawrence (a celebration of Sardinian vegetables), and Alin Laubreaux's *The Happy Glutton*, to name but a few. Then there is her passion for food from start to finish. The purity of the ingredients, the correct utensils, the exquisite presentation of the end result, all are reflected in Elizabeth's instructions. In her recipe for Paella Valenciana, she urges, "The rice should be a beautiful yellow colour, and although moist, each grain should be separate. And if it is necessary to stir, use a fork, not a spoon, which might break the rice."

So concise, but it says it all. Though her recipes are written for cooks (and sometimes require some background or a certain knowledge of technique), their ease, authenticity, and simplicity are the main reason that her work has stood the test of time. Were it not for *A Book of Mediterranean Food*'s excellence as a recipe book, it would long ago have been relegated to the archives as a historical curiosity. I have been a professional bookseller now for almost fifteen years and never a week has gone by when I have not sold several Elizabeth Davids. Even in these days awash with volumes on Mediterranean food, customers will look through them all but buy hers because, as they say, she makes it seem so simple. They are right. I have seen recipes for Scallops à la Provençale that cover two full pages; this is Elizabeth's: "Cut the white part of each scallop into two rounds, season with salt, pepper, and lemon juice, dust with flour, and fry them in butter for a few minutes, put in the coral and a little chopped garlic and parsley, and serve the butter poured over them" (see page 51). No would-be cook would get dinner-party phobias after reading that.

You must remember that at the time this book was written the British regarded foreign food as "filth." Garlic was something abandoned in the Victorian past and Great Britain had managed to impose bad food on a good deal of the globe. Those who read Elizabeth David in the Fifties really couldn't get hold of the ingredients unless they either demanded them or grew them themselves. Customer demand then spread and spread. One is now overwhelmed, even in supermarkets, by exotic vegetables and herbs as well as all manner of oils and vinegars—and garlic is omnipresent. Mediterranean food has become the dominant cuisine in most global cooking, olive oil the elixir of life itself, the tomato the definitive anti-carcinogenic. That vegetables often lack the flavor Elizabeth loved is not her fault. Nowhere in her books did she need to use the words *free range* or *organic*; agribusiness had yet to force their coinage. We now have that hill to reclimb.

I was at the auction sale of Elizabeth's culinary possessions—not so much an auction as a purchase of sacred relics—and was the underbidder on Tom Conran's behalf on the table where she did all her cooking and writing. I watched it go to Prue Leith for a huge sum, a scrubbed old kitchen table. Her bowl of wooden spoons, battered and scarred as one might expect, fetched £400. These bidders weren't dealers; they were people who wanted to be able to say that they owned something that their heroine had used or even just touched. In fact, my most prized possession is her legacy to me, a copy of her favorite book, *The Cookery Book of Lady Clarke of Tillypronie*. Tucked into it is a draft of a page from *English Bread and Yeast Cookery* (1977) so simply written that it keeps me straight when I'm writing recipes.

I didn't know Elizabeth David well, but I remember the first time I answered a phone call from her I dropped the receiver. I told her it was like taking a call from God, and there ever after when she rang me she would announce herself with "God calling." I only met her once, and you could see beneath the ravages of the years the great beauty she once was. At her memorial service at St. Martin-in-the-Fields in London in September 1992, the great of the food world stood and talked of her scholarship and her wit; they talked of the little blue bowl of black olives and the glasses of wine. But no one spoke of her cooking until an aging actor described how she had once prepared him the most perfect of omelettes. Only then could I weep for that woman who had changed all our lives.

—CLARISSA DICKSON WRIGHT

Introduction

*

THE cooking of the Mediterranean shores, endowed with all the natural resources, the colour and flavour of the South, is a blend of tradition and brilliant improvisation. The Latin genius flashes from the kitchen pans.

It is honest cooking, too; none of the sham Grande Cuisine of the International Palace Hotel.

'It is not really an exaggeration', wrote Marcel Boulestin, 'to say that peace and happiness begin, geographically, where garlic is used in cooking.' From Gibraltar to the Bosphorus, down the Rhone Valley, through the great seaports of Marseilles, Barcelona, and Genoa, across to Tunis and Alexandria, embracing all the Mediterranean islands, Corsica, Sicily, Sardinia, Crete, the Cyclades, Cyprus (where the Byzantine influence begins to be felt), to the mainland of Greece and the much disputed territories of Syria, the Lebanon, Constantinople, and Smyrna, stretches the influence of Mediterranean cooking, conditioned naturally by variations in climate and soil and the relative industry or indolence of the inhabitants.

The ever recurring elements in the food throughout these countries are the oil, the saffron, the garlic, the pungent local wines; the aromatic perfume of rosemary, wild marjoram and basil drying in the kitchens; the brilliance of the market stalls piled high with pimentos, aubergines, tomatoes, olives, melons, figs, and limes; the great heaps of shiny fish, silver, vermilion, or tiger-striped, and those long needle fish whose bones so mysteriously turn out to be green. There are, too, all manner of unfamiliar cheeses made from sheep or goat's milk; the butchers' stalls are festooned with every imaginable portion of the inside of every edible animal (anyone who has lived for long in Greece will be familiar with the sound of air gruesomely whistling through sheep's lungs frying in oil).

There are endless varieties of currants and raisins, figs from Smyrna on long strings, dates, almonds, pistachios, and pine kernel nuts, dried melon seeds and sheets of apricot paste which is dissolved in water to make a cooling drink.

All these ingredients make rich and colourful dishes. Over-picturesque, perhaps, for every day; but then who wants to eat the same food every day? I have, therefore, varied this collection with some classic dishes and recipes from regions of France other than those bordering the Mediterranean. I have also devoted a special chapter to dishes which constitute a meal in themselves, such as Paëlla, Cassoulet, and Pilaffs, and another chapter to cold food, fine dishes which are particularly suitable to our servant-less lives; prepared in advance and either preceded or followed by a spicy, aromatic southern dish, what more could one want?

With this selection (it does not claim to be more) of Mediterranean dishes, I hope to give some idea of the lovely cookery of those regions to people who do not already know them, and to stir the memories of those who have eaten this food on its native shores, and who would like sometimes to bring a flavour of those blessed lands of sun and sea and olive trees into their English kitchens.

London, 1950

E. D.

MIDDLE EASTERN COOKERY

A handful of the recipes in this book, learned when I lived in Alexandria, Cairo and Greece, demonstrate the cooking of the Near East. To those who would like to know more of this most interesting and beautiful food I cannot do better than recommend a recently published and comprehensive book on the subject: *Middle Eastern Food* by Claudia Roden (Nelson, 1968).

1969

E. D.

Acknowledgements

****

MY thanks are due to the late Norman Douglas and to his publishers Messrs Chapman & Hall and Messrs Secker and Warburg for permission to include the recipe from *Birds and Beasts of the Greek Anthology* and the extracts from *South Wind* respectively; also to Messrs Faber & Faber for two extracts from *Prospero's Cell* by Lawrence Durrell; to John Lane (The Bodley Head) for a quotation from *The Autobiography of Alice B. Toklas* by Gertrude Stein; to Messrs Hutchinson & Co. for permission to reproduce a passage from *Cross Channel* by Alan Houghton Brodrick; to Messrs William Heinemann and Mrs Frieda Lawrence for the extract from D. H. Lawrence's *Sea and Sardinia*, and also to Messrs Macmillan for the passage from Sir Osbert Sitwell's *Great Morning*; to Messrs Cassell & Co. for permission to quote from Sir Compton Mackenzie's *First Athenian Memories*; to Messrs Edward Arnold for permission to reproduce a recipe from Colonel Kenney-Herbert's *Fifty Luncheons*; to the owner of the copyright of *Things that have Interested Me* by Arnold Bennett; to Mr Innes Rose of John Farquharson Ltd for his permission to include an extract from Henry James's *A Little Tour in France*; to Alfred Knopf Inc. of New York for permission to give the passage from Théophile Gautier's book *Un Voyage en Espagne*, translated into English by Catherine Alison Phillips under the title *A Romantic in Spain*; and to Les Editions Denoel and Messrs Ivor Nicholson & Watson for the passage from *The Happy Glutton* by Alin Laubreaux.

My acknowledgements are also due to the editor and publishers of *Harper's Bazaar*, in which magazine many of the following recipes first appeared.

I should also like to take this opportunity of thanking a number of friends who have most kindly helped me with recipes and with advice, and especially The Hon. Edward Gathorne-Hardy of the British Embassy in Cairo, Mrs Esmat Hammuda of Cairo, and Mr Robin Chancellor for his generous and practical assistance.

Above all I have a debt of gratitude to the late Norman Douglas, whose great knowledge and enchanting talk taught me so much about the Mediterranean.

E.D.

Preface to the 1955 Edition

* *

THIS book first appeared in 1950, when almost every essential ingredient of good cooking was either rationed or unobtainable. To produce the simplest meal consisting of even two or three genuine dishes required the utmost ingenuity and devotion. But even if people could not very often make the dishes here described, it was stimulating to think about them; to escape from the deadly boredom of queuing and the frustration of buying the weekly rations; to read about real food cooked with wine and olive oil, eggs and butter and cream, and dishes richly flavoured with onions, garlic, herbs, and brightly coloured southern vegetables.

In revising the recipes for the present edition I have had little to alter as far as the ingredients were concerned, but here and there I have increased the number of eggs or added a little more stock or bacon or meat to a recipe; I have taken out one or two dishes which were substitute cooking in that, although no false ingredients were used, a good deal of extra seasoning, in the form of tomato purée or wine and vegetables, was added to make up for lack of flavour which should have been supplied by meat or stock or butter.

Because in those days poor quality and lack of ingredients necessitated the use of devious means to achieve the right results, and also because during the last few years I have had opportunities of learning a good deal more than I knew at the time about different methods of cooking, I have been able to simplify the instructions for making some of the dishes. A few recipes which had nothing to do with Mediterranean cooking and which I included perhaps out of over-enthusiasm, I have replaced with Mediterranean recipes which I have since collected. Some of these are for Eastern Mediterranean dishes, from Greece, Syria, Turkey, and the Middle East, others from Italy, Spain, and Provence.

So startlingly different is the food situation now as compared with only two years ago that I think there is scarcely a single ingredient, however exotic, mentioned in this book which cannot be obtained somewhere in this country, even if it is only in one or two shops. Those who make an occasional marketing expedition to Soho or to the region of Tottenham Court Road can buy Greek cheese and Calamata olives, Tahina paste from the Middle East, little birds preserved in oil from Cyprus, stuffed vine leaves from Turkey, Spanish sausages, Egyptian brown beans, chick peas, Armenian ham, Spanish, Italian, and Cypriot olive oil, Italian salame and rice, even occasionally Neapolitan Mozzarella cheese, and honey from Mount Hymettus. These are the details which complete the flavour of a Mediterranean meal, but the ingredients which make this cookery so essentially different from our own are available to all; they are the olive oil, wine, lemons, garlic, onions, tomatoes, and the aromatic herbs and spices which go to make up what is so often lacking in English cooking: variety of flavour and colour, and the warm, rich, stimulating smells of genuine food.

London, 1955

PREFACE TO THE 1965 EDITION

IN the lands bordering the Mediterranean, as indeed almost everywhere else, the cooking is constantly evolving; traditional dishes are being adapted to modern techniques and to new ingredients, or to old ones which, as a result of modern methods of cultivation, transport, preservation, and storage, have undergone material modifications or even a basic change.

In view of these circumstances I have now made, for the 1965 edition of this book, such additions and modifications as were compatible with the character of the original and within its scope.

It is my hope that one day I shall find myself in a position to write a second instalment of this briefest of introductions to the cooking of the Mediterranean shores. In those regions there will always be new discoveries to be made; new doors opening, new impressions to communicate.

January 1965
E. D.

Introduction to the 1988 Edition

* *

WHEN in 1947 I started putting together the recipes which made up this book it was less with any thought of future publication than as a personal antidote to the bleak conditions and acute food shortages of immediate post-war England. Looking back to those days, when meat, butter, cheese, sugar, eggs, bacon, milk, and even biscuits, sweets and chocolate were rationed, when fresh vegetables and fruit were scarce, lemons, oranges and tomatoes as rare as diamonds, commodities such as olive oil, rice, and imported pasta no more than exotic memories, and fresh fish something you stood in a queue for, I see that it was also largely in a spirit of defiance that I wrote down those Mediterranean recipes. I had collected them in Provence, in Corsica, Malta, Athens and the island of Syra in the Cyclades where I had lived for seven months before the Germans overran Greece. Subsequently I had spent a year in Alexandria, where I was employed by the British Admiralty and four or five in Cairo organizing and running a reference library for the British Ministry of Information in the Middle East. Those years, for me good and fruitful, came to an end at Christmas 1945, when I left Egypt to join my husband in New Delhi where he was working on the staff of the Commander-in-Chief, General Auchinleck.

After a few brief months in India, my health in a precarious state, I was returned like a badly wrapped parcel, to England. There I found myself without a job, and with precious little to do except cook. Given the difficulty of finding basic ingredients to put into my pots and pans, it is hardly surprising that shopping for food took up much more time and energy than the actual kitchen preparation and cooking. Still, everybody was in the same boat, and somehow we all managed, even if we did have to eat an awful lot of beans and potatoes, and I had one great advantage over my sisters and friends who had spent the war years in

England. While their store cupboards were stuffed with things like packet soups, dried egg powder, evaporated milk, and crumbling biscuits, I had no such dismal hoards. So I was free to go out looking for anything fit to eat which might be on offer in the shops where ration books and coupons weren't required. That meant greengrocers, fishmongers, and game and poultry dealers. Not an extraordinary choice. It should also be remembered that in those days there were few exotic imports such as now crowd the greengrocery displays. Avocado pears and southern vegetables weren't yet available in England. Aubergines, peppers, courgettes and fennel had hardly been heard of. Even garlic was hard to come by. If you'd mentioned basil or tarragon you'd have been asked who they were.

When in the early autumn of 1946 (I had arrived in England in August) tomatoes reappeared for the first time, things at last seemed to be looking up. I was much mistaken. As autumn turned into winter I shivered in my barely heated top-floor London flat. After living so long in warm climates my wardrobe was absurdly inadequate. Clothes coupons went nowhere. By Christmas real winter had set in. January, February, and March 1947 became memorable as the coldest winter, April as the wettest spring, of the century.

It was during those icy, hungry weeks that I took refuge from reality in writing down memories of the food I had cooked and eaten during my Mediterranean years. As I did so, my remote and at the time rather austere Greek island life began to take on the glow of a lost Paradise of plenty and glamour. As for my war years in Alexandria and Cairo, the food had indeed been plentiful, varied, and often truly delicious. I had of course, although without realizing it, become addicted to the food and cookery of the Mediterranean and the Middle East. That addiction I have never lost. But in the England of the late 1940s and early 1950s it was scarcely possible to indulge it. Well, at least I could put my memories of it on to paper, so that I would not forget about the bright vegetables, the basil, the lemons, the apricots, the rice with lamb and currants and pine nuts, the ripe green figs, the white ewes' milk cheeses of Greece, the thick aromatic Turkish coffee, the herb-scented kebabs, the honey and yoghourt for breakfast, the rose petal jam, the evening ices eaten on an Athenian café terrace in sight of the Parthenon, the unlikely fish stews concocted by a sponge diver from the Dodecanese island of Symi who briefly cooked for me in Alexandria. So it came about that at that particularly bleak and painful period of English gastronomic life immediately following the end of World War II, I put together the bare bones of the book which became *Mediterranean Food*.

Some two years later, in 1949, a friend with connections in the literary world offered to show my ragged collection of recipes —I had after all been using them—to various publishing acquaintances. All of them except one said—and who shall blame them —'What a mad idea writing a cookery book when we don't have enough food to cook.' That one exception was John Lehmann. I didn't know him, although his name was familiar as the editor of Penguin New Writing, when he wrote me a brief note telling me he would like to publish my book, and asking me to go and see him in his Henrietta Street office.

It wasn't only that I had never met John Lehmann. I had never met any publisher and had no idea what to expect. When I was shown into his office, Mr Lehmann was courteous but brisk. He would publish my book, he would pay me £100 advance, £50 on signature of the contract, £50 on publication. He was going to commission John Minton—I hadn't heard of him—to illustrate the book and design the jacket. Mr Lehmann showed me a book about Corsica which he had recently published. It was called *Time Was Away*, and the illustrations and jacket design were by John Minton. The author was Alan Ross. I thought it looked interesting and certainly it was most decorative. So that was settled.

Now about the title. Mr Lehmann wasn't happy with mine. I

had called it *A Book of Mediterranean Food*, but was open to other suggestions. How about *The Blue Train Cookery Book* then? Oh dear. Surely that famous Blue Train had vanished along with our pre-1939 lives and the *Tatler* photographs of society girls sitting in bathing suits on the beaches of Cannes, Menton, Cap d'Antibes, St Juan les Pins? Diffidently, I reached for a straw. 'Er . . . the Blue Train never went to Alexandria and Cairo, did it?' Mr Lehmann agreed that that had been the case. 'Well, have you any other ideas?' he asked. 'I can't help thinking that the word Mediterranean in the title is an important one.' 'Look,' he replied, 'you go home and think about the title, and I'll think about it too, and we'll see what we both come up with. Meanwhile you must write an Introduction to the book and perhaps enlarge it a bit. It's very short, you know.'

Home I went, wondering whatever an Introduction was to be about, and not at all happy at the prospect of thinking up a new title. So it was a tremendous relief when only two or three days later I received a letter from John Lehmann telling me that on reflection he realized that perhaps after all I had been right, and that my original title should stand.

To this day, I admire the good grace with which John, a man who—as I was to discover when I came to know him better—was far from easy-going, conceded that I might have my way over that *Mediterranean Food* title. Now of course it seems unthinkable that it could have been called anything else. At the time, the decision had really been in the balance. As for the Introduction, I produced something pretty perfunctory which Mr Lehmann was tolerant enough to accept. Likewise, my friend Veronica Nicholson, who had talked, not to say nagged, me into turning my notebook of recipes into some semblance of a book, accepted the dedication which I proposed to put in it.

Nowadays, all—or at any rate, nearly all—authors have the assistance of publishers' editors whose task it is to check details of style such as the use of capitals, italics, punctuation and footnotes,

the correct placing of quotation marks, and of course spelling.
(Although I am myself an instinctive good speller, it is surprising
how many writers are hopeless ones.) In the case of cookery
books recipes are scanned for inconsistencies and such aberra-
tions as ingredients which appear in the directions for cooking
the dish but have been forgotten by the author in his initial list
of requirements for it—or in reverse, ingredients left, as it were,
hanging in the air without apparent purpose. All such points are
important in a cookery book, but are often ignored by the cookery writers themselves, as I was to discover when I spent two
years as editor of cookery books for the publishing firm of André
Deutsch. A hazardous job at times. Authors aren't always de-
lighted to have their writing technique questioned. Personally,
I'm only too grateful to have faults and inconsistencies pointed
out, although I do draw the line at so-called editors who go
through my copy adding hundreds of commas and capitals—
you're neurotic about commas, Leonard Russell, literary editor of
the *Sunday Times* in the late 1950s, once told me. No wonder,
given some of the editing I'd been subjected to. Anyway, in 1950
John Lehmann didn't employ a specialist editor to deal with
cookery, so my original typescript (years later John told me it was
the untidiest ever submitted to him) was left more or less as I
had handed it over. Even the recipe for 'Turkish stuffing for a
whole roast sheep' which had so beguiled the late Julia Strachey,
John Lehmann's reader at the time, that, she told me later, she
had finally persuaded John to publish the book on the strength
of it—'Imagine, a whole roast sheep, and the meat ration a few
ounces a week'—was left undisturbed. So was the one for a spit-
roasted *gigot à la provençale*, studded with a dozen cloves of garlic and twice as many anchovy fillets, served with an extra litre
of thrice-blanched cloves of garlic given a fourth and final bath in
a cup of bouillon. That recipe I had chosen to leave—I am no
longer sure why, nor do I remember its source—in the original
French. This elicited a characteristically waspish comment from

8

Mrs Ernestine Carter, the American editor of *Harper's Bazaar*, who by mischance had got her hands on the typescript. Who does she think she is, demanded Mrs Carter of a colleague, does she expect us all to read French? I felt it had been like saying pas devants les domestiques. All the same, I left those French gousses d'ail and filets d'anchois. John Lehmann didn't object to them so why should I translate them for Mrs Carter? They are still there, French and all, on page 77.

In May 1950 *Mediterranean Food* was published. The price was 10s. 6d. John Minton's jacket was stunning. In the shop windows his brilliant blue Mediterranean bay, his tables spread with white cloths and bright fruit, bowls of pasta and rice, a lobster, pitchers and jugs and bottles of wine, could be seen far down the street. On the Sunday following publication day, Elizabeth Nicholas, the immensely respected *Sunday Times* travel writer, published a review of the book. As I read it—I did not then know Mrs Nicholas, although she and I became friends later—I found it hard to believe my eyes. She really liked the book, and she had really read it. Her praise was unqualified, she had understood the reasons that had made me refuse, as she put it, 'to make any ignoble compromises with expediency', adding that it would be the greatest mistake to water down a serious work on Mediterranean food 'to suit present, we hope transitory weaknesses in our own victualling service'. Nicely put, that last phrase. Another point made by Mrs Nicholas, and one which particularly pleased me, was that following well-deserved praise for John Minton's admirable illustrations and a few kind words for my own choice of gastronomic quotation, her final accolade was, 'as further testimony to the unusual quality of this book, it should be added that it contains not one reference to Brillat-Savarin'. It was gratifying that a critic had noticed what had indeed been a very deliberate omission. The great sage of gastronomy had been all very well in his way—and in his day—but it seemed to me that we had all heard rather more than enough of aphorisms like the one about a

9

meal without cheese being like a pretty girl with one eye, and in any case to a generation which had suffered from five years of wartime food and rationing and could barely remember what it had been like to have unlimited butter, cream, oranges, lemons, sugar, jam, meat, not to mention wine and olive oil, the cheese at the end of a meal was an irrelevance. The point was first to make sure you had the wherewithal to prepare a meal, then you could start worrying about whether or not it would be complete without three or four ounces of cheese.

No sooner was *Mediterranean Food* launched than John Lehmann began to ask, 'What can you give me next?' On that occasion I was ready for him. I had a small collection of French recipes which hadn't been suitable for the Mediterranean book. These, when put together, became *French Country Cooking*, again with a jacket design and illustrations by John Minton, and published in 1951. I had made friends with both John Lehmann and John Minton, and it was a blow to me when in 1953, whilst I was half way through the writing of a third book, *Italian Food*, the first John wrote to tell me that his publishing business was to be wound up. Although he had earned much prestige as a high-brow publisher his firm was losing money. The Bristol printers, Purnell's, who had subsidized him and supplied him with paper —still very short in those days—had told him they could no longer finance him. In the course of what must have been an explosive meeting one of the Purnell directors had said, 'What we need, Mr Lehmann, is a few rattling good yarns.' John had stormed out. Perhaps rightly. But he had left his authors desolate. In my case desolation was a firm of publishers called Macdonald's, also owned by Purnell, but financially successful. School books and *Jane's Fighting Ships* were among their assets.

As things turned out, Macdonald's chose to retain only two of John Lehmann's authors. I was one of those unfortunate ones. The other was the American Paul Bowles, author of the much-acclaimed novel *The Sheltering Sky*. Paul, as he told me later, was soon able to shake off his contractual ties with John Lehmann's successors. I was not so lucky.

Sometime in 1954 or 1955 I received an odd letter from one of the Macdonald directors. He realized, he said, that I might find the idea *infra dig.*—strange expression—but Penguin had approached the firm with an offer for *Mediterranean Food* and he felt it his duty to pass it on. So far from thinking a cheap paperback would be '*infra dig.*', I jumped at the offer. A Penguin would mean a vastly increased readership, and in all probability a younger one which would include students, young married couples and many professional women sharing flats or living on their own but still needing to cook for themselves and to give the occasional dinner party. At 10s. 6d. the hardback edition of the book seems and indeed was cheap enough by today's standards but at the time was quite an outlay. The paperback was to be 2s. 6d., a price within the reach of nearly everybody. Children could and did buy the paperback for their parents. More important, in 1954 food rationing had at last come to an end, and apart from Bee Nilson's *The ABC of Cookery* published during the war, there was no other paperback cookery book on the market. My book had been given a dazzling opportunity. It was mainly, I learned, through the efforts of Miss Eunice Frost, the only woman director of Penguin Books, strongly supported by Sir Allen Lane himself, that the offer for *Mediterranean Food* had been made. The remaining members of the board had opposed the project.

Of those disagreements I knew nothing at the time. My task was to revise and update the book, to write some new material, add a few recipes. I was only too pleased to comply with Penguin's modest requests. As I wrote in my preface to their first, 1955, edition, 'So startlingly different is the food situation now as compared with only two years ago that I think there is scarcely a single ingredient, however exotic, mentioned in this book which cannot be obtained somewhere in this country, even if it is only in one or two shops. Those who make an occasional

11

marketing expedition to Soho or to the region of Tottenham Court Road can buy Greek cheese and Calamata olives, Tahina paste from the Middle East, little birds preserved in oil from Cyprus, stuffed vine leaves from Turkey, Spanish sausages, Egyptian brown beans, chick peas, Armenian ham, Spanish, Italian, and Cypriot olive oil, Italian salame and rice, even occasionally Neapolitan Mozzarella cheese, and honey from Mount Hymettus.' How right Elizabeth Nicholas had been about the 'ignoble compromises with expediency' which I had not made. The truth was that I had felt squeamish about compromises. I shrank from words like margarine and vegetable lard. I declined to use those substances in my own cooking, so why inflict them on my readers?

To me it was wonderful that *Mediterranean Food* could now be bought for 2s. 6d., but immensely sad that John Lehmann, who had taken the risk of publishing the book in the first place, had no rights in the paperback—or indeed in any other edition. I resented Macdonald's and the terms they had insisted on for the paperback, although at the time they were, I believe, quite usual. To me that didn't make them any less scandalous. They would get 50% of the royalties, I was to be content with the remaining 50%. So matters remain to this day. That company, which had not had the slightest part in the initial publication of the book—and has never raised a finger to promote it, or either of the subsequent ones which fell into their hands—is still reaping, via the paperback editions, the benefit of John Lehmann's flair and foresight. Macdonald's certainly proved a sorry exchange for John. All that their chief director, a certain Captain Eric Harvey MC, could find to say to me when in 1953 I delivered my typescript of *Italian Food* was, 'Do you mean to say that Mr Lehmann contracted to pay you an advance of £300 for this book? For a *cookery* book? No wonder his firm wasn't paying. Ah well, let's hope we get our money back.'

I am happy to say that although Macdonald's, at the time of

writing part of Captain Robert Maxwell's publishing empire, gather in their share of my paperback royalties, those of the hardback editions have long since passed from their control. Since then the books have gone through several lives, one of them every bit as dismaying as their previous acquisition by Macdonald's. From the hands of a publisher called Robert Hale, of whom I shall say no more than it seemed a singular misfortune to have had my books acquired by his firm, I was rescued by Messrs Dorling Kindersley, the present hardback publishers. I am grateful to them, and hope that this new edition* of my very first book, published thirty-eight years ago, may prosper. I am only sorry that John Lehmann did not live to see it. He died in April 1987, aged 79. Although it now looks so very different, it is still basically the little book he so adventurously published in 1950.

February 1988
E. D.

---

*An illustrated and revised edition was published by Dorling Kindersley in 1988.

Table of Equivalent Gas and Electric Oven Temperatures

Solid Fuel	*Electricity*		*Gas*
Slow	240–310 F.	115–155 C.	¼–2
Moderate	320–370 F.	160–190 C.	3–4
Fairly Hot	380–400 F.	195–205 C.	5
Hot	410–440 F.	210–230 C.	6–7
Very Hot	450–480 F.	235–250 C.	8–9

Table of Equivalent American Measurements

English		*American*
¼ lb butter or fat	=	approx ½ cup solidly packed
2 oz butter or fat	=	approx ¼ cup = 4 tablespoons
1 oz butter or fat	=	approx 2 tablespoons
½ lb caster sugar	=	approx 1 cup plus 3 tablespoons
¼ lb caster sugar	=	approx 8 tablespoons
2 oz caster sugar	=	approx 4 tablespoons
1 lb plain flour sieved	=	approx 4½ cups sieved cake flour
¼ lb plain flour sieved	=	approx 1 cup plus 4 tablespoons
2 oz plain flour sieved	=	approx 8 tablespoons
¼ lb dry grated cheese	=	approx 1 cup
½ lb rice, raw	=	approx 1 cup

LIQUID MEASUREMENTS

English		*American*
1 gallon = 4 quarts = 8 pints	=	10 pints = 1¼ gallons
1 quart = 2 pints = 40 oz	=	2½ pints = 5 cups
1 pint = 20 oz	=	1¼ pints = 2½ cups
½ pint = 10 oz	=	1¼ cups
¼ pint = 5 oz = 1 gill	=	½ cup plus 2 tablespoons
2 oz = 4 tablespoons	=	¼ cup
1 tablespoon = ½ oz	=	½ oz
1 teaspoon = ¼ tablespoon	=	1 teaspoon = ⅓ tablespoon

N.B. Quantities given in the recipes are, unless otherwise stated, for four or five people.

Soups

* * * * * * * * * * * * * * * * * * * *

SOUPE AU PISTOU

The origin of *pistou* is Genoese, but it has become naturalized in
Nice and the surrounding country.

Into 3 pints of boiling water put 1 lb of French beans cut in inch
lengths, 4 medium-sized potatoes, chopped finely, and 3 chopped,
peeled tomatoes. Season with salt and pepper and let them boil
fairly quickly. When the vegetables are almost cooked, throw in
¼ lb of vermicelli and finish cooking gently.

Have ready the following preparation, known as an *aïllade*. In a
mortar pound 3 cloves of garlic, a handful of sweet basil and a
grilled tomato without the skin and pips. When this paste is
thoroughly smooth, add 3 tablespoons of the liquid from the *pistou*.
Pour the *pistou* into a tureen, stir in the *aïllade* and some grated
Gruyère cheese.

SOUPE BASQUE

Brown ¼ lb of chopped onions in lard; add ½ lb of pumpkin cut
in pieces; add the cut-up leaves of a white cabbage, ½ lb previously
soaked dried haricot beans, 2 cloves of garlic, salt and pepper, and
2 quarts of stock or water. Cook 3 hours in a covered pan.

AVGOLÉMONO

The best known of all Greek soups.

To 2 pints of strained chicken broth, add 2 oz rice and boil in
the broth until well cooked. In a basin beat up 2 eggs and the juice
of a lemon. Add a little boiling broth to the eggs in the basin,
spoon by spoon, stirring all the time. Add this to the rest of the
broth and stir for a few minutes over a very slow fire.

SOUPE CATALANE

> 3 large onions, 2 oz chopped ham or bacon, 1 glass white wine,
> 1 small stick celery, 3 tomatoes, 2 potatoes, 2 egg yolks, 3 pints
> stock or water, thyme, parsley, a pinch of nutmeg.

Slice the onions thinly and brown them in olive oil or bacon fat in the pan in which you are going to cook the soup. Stir frequently to prevent them catching. When they start to brown, add the diced ham or bacon, the tomatoes cut in quarters and the chopped celery. Continue stirring for a few minutes, then pour in the glass of wine; let it bubble and then add the stock or water, the potatoes cut in small pieces and the seasoning.

Cook the soup for about 30 minutes. When ready to serve, beat the yolks of eggs with a few spoons of the soup, then pour over the rest of the very hot soup and stir well. Add a good handful of chopped parsley.

The same soup can be made without the egg yolks by adding some vermicelli as soon as the soup has come to the boil; or make it without any thickening and serve with grated cheese.

PURÉE LÉONTINE

> 2 lb leeks, 1 cup each of spinach, green peas, and shredded lettuce,
> 1 tablespoon each of chopped parsley, mint, and celery, ½ tumbler
> olive oil, lemon juice, salt, and pepper.

Clean and cut the leeks into chunks. Into a thick marmite put the olive oil and when it is warm put in the leeks, seasoned with salt, pepper, and the lemon juice. Simmer slowly for about 20 minutes. Now add the spinach, the peas, and the lettuce, stir a minute or two, and add a quart of water. Cook until all the vegetables are soft – about 10 minutes – then press the whole mixture through a sieve. If the purée is too thick add a little milk, and before serving stir in the chopped parsley, mint, and celery.

This soup turns out an appetizing pale green. Enough for six people.

SOUP OF HARICOT BEANS

With the remains of a Cassoulet (p. 102) a most delicious soup can be made.

Heat up the beans which are left over in a little extra water, and pound them through a sieve. Reheat the purée, adding sufficient stock and a little milk to thin down the soup, and put in some pieces of sausage cut in dice.

SOUP WITH RISOTTO

For using left-over Risotto (p. 93).

Make the rice into little balls the size of a nut. Egg and bread-crumb them and fry them in butter, and when they are dry add them to any kind of hot soup – chicken broth, for instance, or a simple vegetable soup.

POTAGE DE TOPINAMBOURS À LA PROVENÇALE

Cook 2 lb of Jerusalem artichokes in 3 pints of salted water. Sieve, and heat up, adding gradually ½ pint of milk.

In a small frying pan heat 2 tablespoons of olive oil and in this fry two chopped tomatoes, a clove of garlic, a small piece of chopped celery, a little parsley and 2 tablespoons of chopped ham or bacon. Let this mixture cook only a minute or two, then pour it, with the oil, into the soup. Heat, and serve quickly.

HOT CUCUMBER SOUP

1 lb potatoes, 2 large onions, 2 whole cucumbers, milk, parsley, chives, 1 pickled cucumber, leek tops, mint, salt, and pepper.

Boil the potatoes and 1 onion in water. When they are soft pass through a sieve and proceed as for potato soup, making a thin smooth purée with the milk. Grate into this soup 2 whole unpeeled cucumbers, 1 raw onion, add the pickled cucumber cut into small pieces, and all the other ingredients chopped fine, and reheat cautiously, so that the vinegar in the pickled cucumber does not curdle the milk.

ZUPPA DI PESCE

There are many versions of fish soup in Italy, and most of them are, like the Bouillabaisse, more of a stew than a soup. The varieties of bony and spiny fish used in the Genoese *burrida*, the Livornese *cacciucco*, and the Neapolitan *zuppa di pesce* are much the same as in a Bouillabaisse (see p. 59), but with the addition of squid cut in rings, small clams called *vongole*, sometimes small red mullet, prawns, mussels, small lobsters or *langouste*.

The basis of Italian fish soups is usually a broth made with oil and tomato, flavoured with garlic, onion, and herbs, sometimes dried mushrooms, sometimes white wine or a little vinegar. In this broth the fish are cooked and served, accompanied by slices of French bread baked in the oven.

A very simple version of an Italian fish soup can be made with mussels, and prawns. To make the broth, put 2 or 3 tablespoons of olive oil in a wide, heavy pan. When it has warmed put in a small chopped onion; let it melt a little, add a tablespoon each of chopped celery leaves and parsley and a clove or two of garlic. Cook a minute then add 1 lb of chopped and skinned tomatoes. Simmer until the tomatoes are reduced to a sauce. Add a small glass of white wine and the same amount of water. Season rather highly with pepper, and if you like a little cayenne, and a very little salt. If the broth is too thick add a little more water. In this preparation cook 4 pints of cleaned mussels and 1 pint of large prawns (these *should* be in their shells and uncooked, although personally I do not care for the very strong flavour which the prawn shells give to the soup, and I usually buy cooked prawns and shell them before adding them).* If you are using Dublin Bay prawns, use the tails only and slit the shells down the centre before putting them into the pan, to facilitate shelling when they are served. (Dublin Bay prawn shells have nothing like the strong flavour of those of ordinary prawns.)

As soon as the mussels have all opened sprinkle a little chopped parsley and if you like a little lemon juice or chopped lemon peel

* In this case use half the quantity.

20

over the top, and serve at once in very hot soup plates, with slices of bread baked in the oven. For those who like it, rub the slices of baked bread with a cut clove of garlic before serving.

Another way of making a simplified *zuppa di pesce* is to cook slices of any fish such as red or grey mullet, mackerel, brill, whiting, haddock, or gurnard in the prepared tomato broth, then add the mussels and prawns, but in half the quantities given. Those who don't like fishing bones out of the soup can use filleted fish.

A MEDITERRANEAN FISH SOUP

A cod's head, a cooked crawfish, 2 pints cockles or mussels, 1 pint prawns, 1 pimento, 1½ lb tomatoes, a lemon, a few celery leaves, a carrot, 2 onions, 6 cloves of garlic, 3 tablespoons rice, coarse salt, ground black pepper, thyme, marjoram, basil, fennel, parsley, a piece of orange peel, ½ pint white wine, 4 pints water, saffron, parsley.

Make a stock with the cod's head, the shells of the crawfish and the prawns, the celery, onions, carrot, a slice each of lemon and orange peel, marjoram, thyme, white wine and water, and a tea-spoonful of saffron. Simmer this stock for an hour.

In the meantime chop the tomatoes and put them to cook in a thick pan with the pimento and a clove of garlic, and a very little olive oil, simmering them until reduced to a purée.

Clean the mussels or cockles and open them in a very little water over a quick fire; take them out of their shells and strain the liquid through a muslin.

When the stock has cooked, strain it, return it to the pan; bring it to the boil, put in the rice and simmer it for 15 minutes; now add, through a sieve, the tomatoes; the crawfish cut into small pieces, the whole prawns, and stock from the mussels or cockles. Let all this heat together for 5 minutes; by this time the soup should be of a fairly thick and creamy consistency. As the soup bubbles and is ready to serve stir in a handful of fresh parsley, basil, or fennel, the mussels or cockles, a dessertspoon of grated lemon peel and a small clove of garlic crushed in a mortar. Another minute and the soup is ready. The addition of the herbs, the lemon, and the garlic at the last moment gives the soup its fresh flavour.

WHITE FISH SOUP

2 lb any firm white fish, 1 cod's head, 1 onion, 1 leek, celery, garlic, parsley, 3 tablespoons tomato purée, 1 glass white wine, 1 cup milk, a few sprigs of fennel, lemon peel, flour.

Put the fish and vegetables into a pan and cover with water. When the fish is cooked, remove it carefully, taking out any bones, cut in large pieces, and keep it aside. Continue cooking the rest of the stock for 20 minutes. Then strain it through a sieve and return to the pan. Add the white wine, the tomato purée; thicken with 2 tablespoons of flour stirred in a cup of milk and poured into the soup through a strainer when it is off the boil.

When the soup is smooth (it should not be very thick) put in the pieces of cooked fish, add a large handful of coarsely chopped parsley, the chopped fennel, and chopped lemon peel. There should be at least one large piece of fish for each plate of soup. Serve with slices of toasted French bread.

SOUPE AUX MOULES

2 pints mussels, 1 small onion, 1 stick celery, 1 clove of garlic, 1 glass white wine, parsley, lemon, 2 eggs.

Cook the mussels as for *moules marinière* (p. 51). When they have opened, take them out of their shells and keep them aside. Strain the liquid in which they have cooked through muslin (there is always a little sand or grit deposited from the mussels, however carefully they have been cleaned).

Heat up this stock, put back the shelled mussels and a handful of chopped parsley and cook 2 minutes more. The less the mussels are re-cooked, once they have been shelled, the better they will be. Beat up the eggs in a bowl with a little lemon juice, pour some of the stock into it, stir well, return the mixture to the pan, and continue stirring until the soup is hot, but it must not boil.

TOMATO AND SHELL-FISH SOUP

This is typical of the way many soups are made in Mediterranean countries. Sometimes French beans are added or potatoes cut in dice.

> 1 lb onions, 2 lb tomatoes, a sherry glass olive oil, herbs and seasoning, garlic, 1 breakfast cup of any cooked shell fish (mussels, prawns, clams, or *scampi*), 1 oz vermicelli, parsley.

Heat the olive oil in a thick pan and put in the sliced onions and let them cook slowly until they are melted and golden. Now add the tomatoes, chopped roughly, salt, pepper, herbs, and a clove or two of garlic, and let the whole mixture simmer until the tomatoes are soft.

Now add 1½ pints of water or stock from the shell fish. Cook slowly for 20 to 30 minutes. Put the soup through a sieve.

Return it to the pan, bring it to the boil and throw in the vermicelli in very small pieces and whatever shell fish you are using. In 5 minutes it will be ready. Add chopped parsley before serving.

MELOKHIA

Melokhia is a glutinous soup much beloved by the Arabs, particularly in Egypt. *Melokhia* is a kind of mallow (Greek *malakhe*, Latin *malva*).

> 1 lb green *melokhia*, 3 glasses rabbit stock, several cloves of garlic, a tablespoon of coriander seeds, salt, and *shatta* (ground dried chillies) or cayenne pepper.

Wash the *melokhia* well and drain it until dry. Take the green leaves only and chop them finely – this is done with the two-handled chopper called a *makhrata*.* Put the stock into a pan and heat it. When it is boiling add half the coriander and garlic pounded together. Add the chopped *melokhia* and stir it well for a minute or

---

* *Hâchoir* in French, *mezzaluna* in Italian. These instruments can now be bought at a few good kitchen stores (William Page, Shaftesbury Avenue, Staines of Victoria Street, Cadec, 27 Greek Street, Soho, etc.). Once you have used one, it is unthinkable to be without it.

two, and remove the pan from the fire. Fry the rest of the pounded coriander and garlic in hot fat and add it to the *melokhia*, with the *shatta* or cayenne. Leave the casserole uncovered on a low flame for a few minutes. This is served in a soup plate, accompanied by another plate of boiled rice with rabbit or chicken.

ICED CUCUMBER JELLY SOUP

Grate 2 large cucumbers with the peel. Add half a small onion grated, lemon juice, salt, pepper, and some very finely chopped mint. Stir in about ½ pint of melted aspic jelly (see p. 141) and leave to set. Garnish each cup of soup with a few prawns.

GASPACHO

Gaspacho, the popular iced Spanish soup, was described, some-what disparagingly, by Théophile Gautier after a journey to Spain in 1840; like all good Frenchmen he was apt to be suspicious of foreign food.

'Our supper was of the simplest kind; all the serving men and maids of the hostelry had gone to the dance, and we had to be content with a mere gaspacho. This gaspacho is worthy of a special description, and we shall here give the recipe, which would have made the hair of the late Brillat-Savarin stand on end. You pour some water into a soup tureen, and to this water you add a dash of vinegar, some cloves of garlic, some onions cut into quarters, some slices of cucumber, a few pieces of pimento, a pinch of salt; then one cuts some bread and sets it to soak in this pleasing mixture, serving it cold. At home, a dog of any breeding would refuse to sully its nose with such a compromising mixture. It is the favourite dish of the Andalusians, and the prettiest women do not shrink from swallowing bowlfuls of this hell-broth of an evening. Gaspacho is considered highly refreshing, an opinion which strikes me as rather rash, but, strange as it may seem the first time one tastes it, one ends by getting used to it and even liking it. As a most providen-tial compensation we had a decanter of an excellent dry white

Malaga wine to wash down this meagre repast, and drained it conscientiously to the last drop, thus restoring our strength, exhausted by a nine hours' spell upon indescribable roads at a temperature like that of a kiln.'*

Modern versions of *gaspacho* appear to be very different from the hell-broth described by Gautier. The basis of them is chopped tomato, olive oil, and garlic, and there may be additions of cucumber, black olives, raw onion, red pepper, herbs, eggs, and bread. The following makes a very good and refreshing *gaspacho*.

Chop a pound of raw peeled tomatoes until they are almost in a purée. Stir in a few dice of cucumber, 2 chopped cloves of garlic, a finely sliced spring onion, a dozen stoned black olives, a few strips of green pepper, 3 tablespoons of olive oil, a tablespoon of wine vinegar, salt, pepper, and a pinch of cayenne pepper, a little chopped fresh marjoram, mint, or parsley. Keep very cold until it is time to serve the soup, then thin with ½ pint of iced water, add a few cubes of coarse brown bread, and serve with broken-up ice floating in the bowl. A couple of hard-boiled eggs, coarsely chopped, make a good addition. Sometimes these, plus a selection of the vegetables – the cucumber, olives, peppers, onions – and the bread, are finely chopped and handed round separately in small dishes instead of being incorporated in the basic soup.

Sometimes *gaspacho* is presented in large deep cups, sometimes in shallow soup plates.

ICED CHICKEN AND TOMATO CONSOMMÉ

For 1 pint of chicken stock take ¼ pint of fresh (or canned) tomato juice and cook for 5 minutes with a clove of garlic, 2 lumps of sugar, salt, pepper, and basil. Strain and add the chicken consommé and a glass of white wine. Heat again and then chill in the ice box.

---

* *Un Voyage en Espagne*, translated by Catherine Alison Phillips, and published by Alfred A. Knopf, under the title of *A Romantic in Spain*.

ICED BEETROOT SOUP

Cook 4 large beetroots in the oven, exactly as for potatoes baked in their jackets – they will take 2 or 3 hours, and the resulting delicious flavour happily bears no resemblance to the bloodless things sold ready cooked by the greengrocers. Peel them and grate them into 2 pints of aspic jelly (p. 141), add a little vinegar and seasoning and heat this mixture gently for 10 minutes, then pour it through a sieve. The liquid should be a strong clear red. Put it into a bowl to set. To serve, put a cold poached egg into the bottom of each shallow soup bowl and pile the jellied beetroot on top in spoonfuls. Iced soup ought not to be served in a set piece or it looks like a nursery jelly.

OKROCHKA

There are many variations of *okrochka*, and it can be made with different kinds of fish, fish and meat mixed, or simply with pieces of cold cooked chicken. The essential ingredients are the fresh and pickled cucumbers and the fennel which gives it its characteristic flavour.

The *okrochka* which I enjoyed many times at the Russian Club in Athens was made with *kwass** and yoghourt was served separately. Here is a recipe which can quite easily be made in England. It is a filling soup and should be served in small quantities, when it makes a refreshing first dish on a hot evening.

> 1 cup diced fresh cucumber, ½ cup diced frankfurter sausage or cold chicken, ¼ cup cooked shrimps or lobster, 2 tablespoons each of chopped green onion tops, fennel leaves, pickled cucumber, and parsley, 2 hard-boiled eggs, ¼ pint yoghourt, 1 cup of milk, salt, and freshly ground black pepper.

Mix the milk into the yoghourt to thin it down, then add all the other ingredients except the hard-boiled eggs. Leave on the ice at least 2 hours, and before serving put a cube or two of ice into each

---

* A Russian fermented liquor.

cup, and some chopped hard-boiled egg, and sprinkle over some more parsley.

ICED PIMENTO SOUP

From a small tin of red Spanish pimentos (preferably the roasted kind) mash half into a purée and cook a few minutes with twice the quantity of tomato juice. Add the rest of the pimentos cut in strips, and ice. If fresh pimentos are used, grill, skin, seed, and pound them before mixing with the tomato. Very fine slices of raw pimento can be used for garnishing.

Eggs and Luncheon Dishes

Eggs and Luncheon Dishes

Henry James's Luncheon at Bourg

* * * * * * * * * * * * * * * * * * * *

'THE well-fed Bressois are surely a good-natured people. I call them well-fed both on general and on particular grounds. Their province has the most savoury aroma, and I found an opportunity to test its reputation. I walked back into the town from the church (there was really nothing to be seen by the way), and as the hour of the midday breakfast had struck, directed my steps to the inn. The table d'hôte was going on, and a gracious, bustling, talkative landlady welcomed me. I had an excellent repast – the best repast possible – which consisted simply of boiled eggs and bread and butter. It was the quality of these simple ingredients that made the occasion memorable. The eggs were so good that I am ashamed to say how many of them I consumed. "La plus belle fille du monde", as the French proverb says, "ne peut donner que ce qu'elle a"; and it might seem that an egg which has succeeded in being fresh has done all that can reasonably be expected of it. But there was a bloom of punctuality, so to speak, about these eggs of Bourg, as if it had been the intention of the very hens themselves that they should be promptly served. "Nous sommes en Bresse, et le beurre n'est pas mauvais," the landlady said with a sort of dry coquetry, as she placed this article before me. It was the poetry of butter, and I ate a pound or two of it; after which I came away with a strange mixture of impressions of late gothic sculpture and thick *tartines*.'

A Little Tour in France
by Henry James

THE SAVOURY OMELETTE

Egg dishes and omelettes are the perfect dishes for small luncheons. Everyone has favourite recipes for these, so I have only included a very few.

As far as omelettes are concerned I cannot do better than to quote 'Wyvern's' wholly admirable views on the subject:

'The recipe for this *omelette* differs somewhat from those usually propounded, being that of the *cuisinière bourgeoise* rather than that of

31

the *Chef*. The latter looks very nice, and is often finished tastefully with a pattern skilfully wrought with glaze, *cordons* of *purées* and other decoration. To my mind the *omelette* suffers in being made so pretty, and is not as good a thing to eat as that of roadside inn or *cabaret*.

'An *omelette* ought never to be stiff enough to retain a very neatly rolled up appearance. If cooked with proper rapidity it should be too light to present a fixed form, and on reaching the hot dish should spread itself, rather, on account of the delicacy of its substance. Books that counsel you to *turn* an *omelette*, to fold it, to let it brown on one side, to let it fry for about five minutes, etc., are not to be trusted. If you follow such advice you will only produce, at best, a neat looking egg pudding.

'Timed by the seconds hand of a watch, an *omelette* of six eggs, cooked according to my method "by the first intention", takes forty five seconds from the moment of being poured into the pan to that of being turned into the dish.

'Though cream is considered by some to be an improvement, I do not recommend it. Milk is certainly a mistake, for it makes the *omelette* leathery. I confess that I like a very little minced chives in all savoury *omelettes*; but this is a matter of taste. Finely chopped parsley should be added with a seasoning of salt and pepper. The general rules to be observed in *omelette* making, according to my process, then, may be thus summed up:

'1. Mix thoroughly but do not *beat* the eggs, and never use more than six for one *omelette*, omitting two of the whites.

'2. It is better to make two of six than one of twelve eggs. Success is *impossible* if the vessel be too full. If using four eggs omit one white.

'3. Three eggs mixed whole make a nice sized *omelette*, quite the best for the beginner to commence with.

'4. Use a proper utensil, rather shallow, with narrow, well sloping sides; a twelve inch fireproof china pan will be found excellent; see that it is clean and quite dry.

'5. Do not overdo the amount of butter that you use for the

frying – enough to lubricate the pan evenly to the extent of a quarter of an inch is sufficient.

'6. Be sure that your pan is *ready* to receive your mixture. If not hot enough your *omelette* will be leathery, or you will have to mix it in the pan like scrambled eggs (*œufs brouillés*).

'7. The moment the butter ceases to fizz and turns brownish, the moisture having been expelled, the pan is ready.

'8. Pour the mixture into the pan so that it may spread well over the lubricated surface, then instantly lift up the part of the *omelette* that sets at the moment of contact, and let the unformed portion run under it; repeat this two or three times if the pan be at all full, keep the left hand at work with a gentle see-saw motion to encourage rapidity in setting, give a finishing shake, and turn the *omelette* into the hot dish *before* the whole of the mixture on the surface has quite set.

'9. The *omelette*, slightly assisted by the spoon, will roll over almost of its own accord if the sides of the pan be sloped as I have described, burying within it the slightly unformed juicy part of the mixture which remained on the surface; it will not require folding.

'10. Three-quarters of a minute is ample time for the whole operation, if the pan be properly hot when the mixture is poured into it, and the heat evenly maintained.

'11. Have the hot dish close by the fire, so that you can turn the *omelette* into it *instanter*. A little melted butter, with some chopped parsley and chives, may, with advantage, be put into the dish.

'12. It is above all things necessary to have a brisk fire under the pan while the *omelette* is being cooked. A fair-sized gas boiler serves the purpose. The small three-egg *omelette* can be made successfully over a powerful methylated spirit lamp. The ordinary kitchen fire is unsuited for this work unless it can be brought up level with the hot plate, with a clear live coal surface.

'As it lies in the dish this *omelette* will not look like a bolster – it will take a natural, rather flat, irregular oval shape, golden yellow in colour, and flecked with green, with the juicy part escaping from beneath its folds.'*

* *Fifty Luncheons*, by A. Kenney-Herbert.

Colonel Kenney-Herbert's 'twelve-inch fireproof china pan' would be difficult to come by nowadays, but there are plenty of substitutes, and even heavy iron omelette pans *can*, with trouble, be found in England.

ETIQUETTE

Regarding the world of subtlety which can be infused into the serving of a dish of eggs, I cannot resist quoting here the lucid opinion of a French cook, as related by Gertrude Stein.

'The dinner was cooked by Hélène. I must tell a little about Hélène.

'Hélène had already been three years with Gertrude Stein and her brother. She was one of those admirable bonnes, in other words excellent maids of all work, good cooks thoroughly occupied with the welfare of their employers and of themselves, firmly convinced that everything purchasable was far too dear. "Oh, but it is dear!" was her answer to any question. She wasted nothing and carried on the household at the regular rate of 8 francs a day. She even wanted to include guests at that price, it was her pride, but of course that was difficult since she for the honour of her house as well as to satisfy her employers always had to give everyone enough to eat. She was a most excellent cook and she made a very good soufflé. In those days most of the guests were living more or less precariously; no one starved, someone always helped, but still most of them did not live in abundance. It was Braque who said about four years later when they were all beginning to be known, with a sigh and a smile, "How life has changed! We all now have cooks who can make a soufflé."

'Hélène had her opinions; she did not, for instance, like Matisse. She said a Frenchman should not stay unexpectedly to a meal, particularly if he asked the servant beforehand what there was for dinner. She said foreigners had a perfect right to do these things but not a Frenchman, and Matisse had once done it. So when Miss Stein said to her, "Monsieur Matisse is staying for dinner this evening," she would say, "In that case I will not make an *omelette* but fry the eggs. It takes the same number of eggs and the same amount of butter but it shows less respect, and he will understand." '*

TARTE À L'OIGNON ET AUX ŒUFS

7 oz flour, 2 oz butter, 1½ oz lard, ¼ tumbler water, salt.

Make a paste with all the ingredients and spread it in a buttered flan dish.

Have ready the following preparation:

Put 1½ lb of onions into boiling salted water and cook them until they are reduced to a purée. Mix this purée with a large cup of rather thick *béchamel* (p. 182).

Spread the mixture on the uncooked pastry. Arrange more strips of pastry criss-cross over the onions and bake about 45 minutes.

Serve with poached eggs on top.

RATATOUILLE AUX ŒUFS

1 lb potatoes, ¾ lb onions, 2 cloves of garlic, 3 small marrows, 3 tomatoes, 3 green pimentos, eggs, olive oil, lard.

Clean all the vegetables and cut them into rounds. Into a heavy frying pan put half a glass of oil and 2 tablespoons of lard; put in the vegetables, season with salt and pepper, and simmer with the pan covered for 45 minutes, and another 30 minutes without the lid.

Turn into a serving dish and place on top a fried egg for each person.

ŒUFS EN MATELOTE

Cook ½ pint of red wine with herbs, onion, garlic, salt and pepper. Boil for 3 minutes and take out the herbs. In the wine poach 6 eggs, put them on slices of fried bread rubbed with garlic. Quickly reduce the sauce and thicken it with butter worked with flour and pour over the eggs.

* *The Autobiography of Alice B. Toklas*, by Gertrude Stein.

CHATCHOUKA

A Tunisian dish.

6 small green pimentos, 8 tomatoes, 4 eggs, butter or olive oil.

Remove the cores and seeds from the pimentos, and cut them in strips. Heat a little oil or butter in a shallow earthenware dish. In this stew the pimentos, and add the tomatoes, whole, when the pimentos are half cooked. Season with salt and pepper. When the tomatoes are soft, break in the eggs, whole, and cover the pan until they are cooked. Serve in the dish in which they have cooked. Sometimes a little chopped or minced chicken or meat is cooked with the pimentos, sometimes onions, and sometimes the Chatchouka is cooked in individual earthenware egg dishes.

HUEVOS AL PLATO A LA BARCINO

A Spanish dish.

6 eggs, ¼ lb of leg of pork, 2 oz ham, 2 oz butter, ½ lb tomatoes, 1 oz flour, an onion, a little stock.

Slice the onion, the ham, and the pork into small strips; let them melt in the butter; when they have turned golden stir in the flour, add the chopped tomatoes and about ¼ pint of meat stock. Simmer this sauce gently for 20 minutes or so, until it is very thick, and season with pepper and salt. Turn it into a fireproof egg dish, break in the eggs, and cook in the oven until the whites have set.

OMELETTE AU BROCCIU

Brocciu is the Corsican cheese made of ewe-milk which gives a characteristic salty tang to many Corsican dishes.

The eggs and cheese are beaten up together, with the addition of chopped wild mint, and made into a flat round omelette.

OMELETTE AUX MOULES

Prepare a mixture of onion lightly browned in olive oil, flavoured with garlic, parsley, and a little white wine.

Add the cooked shelled mussels to this, and at the appropriate moment add them to your omelette, which is served with a little tomato sauce in addition.

MOUSAKÁ

A dish well known all over the Balkans, Turkey, and the Middle East. This is the Greek version.

First prepare a thick batter by cooking together 2 beaten egg yolks and ½ pint of milk, seasoned with salt and pepper, until it is like a very solid custard. Leave to cool.

Mince 1 lb of cooked beef or lamb very fine. Fry 3 large sliced onions in oil till brown. Cut 3 or 4 unpeeled aubergines into large slices and fry in hot oil.

Put some more oil into a deep square or oblong cake tin* and cover the bottom with aubergines; cover the aubergines with the minced meat, and this with the fried onions. Repeat till all the ingredients are in the dish. Then put in ½ cup each of meat stock and fresh tomato sauce, cover with the prepared batter mixture and put the dish in a moderate oven (gas no. 4) for about an hour. The batter should form a kind of crust on the top of the *mousaká*, and should be golden brown. Usually served hot, but also very good cold. Can also be reheated very successfully.

TARTE AUX TOMATES

Make a pastry with ½ lb of flour, ¼ lb of butter, an egg, and a pinch of salt.

Line a shallow tin with the pastry, and pour into it a thick *béchamel* sauce (p. 182) into which you have incorporated 2 table-spoons of concentrated tomato purée. On top of this put some stoned black olives and some chicken livers which have been chopped and sautéd in butter for 2 or 3 minutes. Cover with a layer of tomatoes cut in half and grilled for a couple of minutes. Bake in a moderate oven until the pastry is cooked.

* The quantities given fill a cake tin 6½ inches square and 2 inches deep.

SCALOPPINE OF CALF'S LIVER WITH PIMENTOS

> 1 lb calf's liver cut in thin slices, 4 sweet red pimentos, a small wine glass white wine, lemon juice, salt, pepper, a little flour, olive oil.

Prepare the pimentos by putting them under the grill and turning them round until their skins have blackened. When they have cooled, rub off the skins, remove the core and seeds, wash them in cold water, and cut into strips.

Season the slices of liver with salt, pepper, and lemon juice. Dust them lightly with flour. Put them into a frying pan in which you have heated half a coffeecupful of olive oil, and sauté them quickly on both sides; pour over the white wine (keep out of the way of the sizzling oil), let it bubble, add the pimentos, and cook gently another 5 minutes.

ROGNONS BRAISÉS AU PORTO

The beauty of this dish depends on the aroma of the truffle permeating the wine and the kidneys, and the pan must be kept carefully covered during the cooking.

Cut 1 lb veal kidneys in slices. Put in a shallow sauté pan with 1 onion cut up, salt, pepper, a piece of lemon peel, a bay leaf, and a sliced truffle. Cover with half water and half port. Cover the pan and stew very slowly for about 1½ hours. Add some mushrooms already sautéd in butter, thicken the sauce with a little flour or cream, and cook another 10 minutes.

LANGUE DE BŒUF EN PAUPIETTES

Remove the horny part from an ox tongue; blanch it in boiling water for 15 minutes and then cook in a casserole until the skin can be removed. When cold cut in thin slices and cover each piece with a layer of meat stuffing; paint over with a knife dipped in beaten egg to unify the stuffing, roll the slices, put a small piece of bacon on each and tie up or pierce with a skewer. These should be roasted in front of the fire but can be cooked in the oven in a casserole. When they are almost cooked sprinkle breadcrumbs over the paupiettes, and when they are a golden brown serve with a sauce *piquante* (p. 186).

PISSALADINA *or* PISSALADIÈRE

This dish is one of the delights of Marseilles, Toulon, and the Var country, where it is sold in the market places and the bakeries in the early morning and can be bought, piping hot, by the slice, off big iron trays.

Get from the baker a piece of uncooked bread, pull it out and spread a baking sheet with it. Cover the bottom of a saucepan with olive oil. Add 2 lb of sliced onions; do not brown them but let them slowly melt almost to a purée, which will take about 40 minutes. Pour the purée on to the dough, put stoned black olives on the top and decorate it with criss-cross fillets of anchovy. Cook in the oven.

If bread dough is unobtainable, an excellent dish can be made by spreading the onion purée into a tin lined with the same pastry as for the *tarte à l'oignon* (p. 35) or thick slices of bread cut length-ways from a sandwich loaf. Fry one side lightly in olive oil, spread this side with the purée, put in a tin in the oven with a little more oil and cook about 10 minutes.

The flavour of the olive oil is essential to this dish.

Further along the coast, across the Italian border, these dishes baked on bread dough are called *pizza*, which simply means a pie, and there are many variations of them, the best known being the Neapolitan *pizza* which consists of tomatoes, anchovies, and mozzarella cheese (a white buffalo-milk cheese). The local *pizza* of San Remo is very like the Provençal *pissaladière*, but garnished with salted sardines instead of anchovies; it is known locally as *sardenara*.

If you can get yeast from a local bakery which makes its own bread, the dough for a *pizza* or a *pissaladière* can be made as follows: dissolve a little under ¼ oz of yeast in a little tepid water; pour ¼ lb of plain flour in a mound on a pastry board; make a well in the centre, put in the yeast and a teaspoonful of salt. Fold the flour over the yeast, and blend all together. Add about ⅛ pint of water and knead to a stiff dough. Press the dough out and away from you with the palm of the hand, holding the dough with the other hand. When the dough begins to feel light and springy roll it into a ball, put it on a floured plate, cover with a floured cloth, and leave in a warm place for 2 to 3 hours, by which time it should have risen, and doubled in volume.

To make the *pissaladière* roll out the dough into a large disc or square (about ¼ inch thick) and garnish it with the onions, black olives, and anchovies, prepared as already explained, and bake in a fairly hot oven for 20 to 30 minutes.

ANCHOÏADE

There are several versions of this Provençal dish.

The one I know (and like best) is made in much the same way as *pissaladina*, but instead of the onion mixture the uncooked dough is spread with a mixture of anchovies, tomatoes half cooked in olive oil and highly flavoured with garlic and basil, and then baked in the oven.

Here is Reboul's recipe for *anchoïade*. 'Soak some fillets of anchovies in water for a few minutes to remove the salt. Place them in a dish with some olive oil, a pinch of pepper and 2 or 3 cloves of garlic cut up. You can also add a drop of vinegar. Cut the crust lengthways off a whole long loaf, about an inch thick, and cut this in pieces so that there is one for each guest; on each put some fillets of anchovy, and put each slice on a plate.

'Cut some more slices of bread in squares. Each person soaks his slice alternately in the prepared oil and anchovy mixture in the dish and then crushes it down on the anchovies and bread in his own plate. When all is finished, anchovies and sauce, the pieces of bread which remain are toasted before the fire. There results a characteristic aroma which rejoices every *amateur* of Provençal cooking, and is the delight of many gastronomes.'

Another way of serving *anchoïade* is to spread the prepared mixture of olive oil, garlic, and anchovies on pieces of toast and heat them in the oven.

ANCHOÏADE CROZE*

Rolls cut in two and filled with a purée made of brined anchovies, almonds or walnuts, figs, onions, garlic, savoury herbs, tarragon, fennel seed, red pimento, olive oil, lemon and orange-blossom water; baked and served with black olives.

ÉPINARDS EN BOUILLABAISSE

Cook 2 lb of cleaned spinach in water for 5 minutes. Drain it and press out all the water, and chop it.

Into a large shallow pan put 3 or 4 dessertspoons of oil and a chopped onion. After a minute or two add the spinach and stir over a slow fire for 5 minutes, then add 5 or 6 raw potatoes cut in thin slices; the waxy kind are best for this dish as they are less likely to disintegrate.

Season with salt, pepper, and a pinch of saffron; pour over about 1½ pints of boiling water, add 2 cloves of garlic chopped, and a branch of fennel, and simmer with the lid on until the potatoes are cooked. At this moment break into the pan 1 egg for each person and cook gently.

Into each guest's plate put a slice of bread and with a ladle carefully take out an egg (they should be *poached*) and a portion of the vegetables, and place it on the slice of bread, with some of the *bouillon*.

From Reboul's *La Cuisinière Provençale*

BUREK

Burek are little pastries filled either with a mixture of spinach or fresh cream cheese flavoured with mint. They are of Turkish origin. The pastry used is called '*fila*', which is something like flaky pastry, rolled out very thinly. In Greece, Turkey, and Egypt it can be bought ready-made and looks like sheets of paper. In London

---

* Austin de Croze.

fila pastry can be bought from John and Pascalis, 35 Grafton Way, Tottenham Court Road, and from the Hellenic Provision Stores, 25 Charlotte Street.

For *burek* cut the pastry into 2-inch squares, put a spoonful of spinach purée, or fresh cream cheese beaten with an egg and a little chopped mint in the centre of each one and fold the pastry over so that it is triangular shaped. Fry them in plenty of hot oil or dripping.

SPANAKOPITTÁ

This is a Greek (and also Turkish) dish made with the same *fila* pastry as the *burek*.

   3 oz *fila* pastry leaves, 2 lb spinach, 3 oz butter, ¼ lb Gruyère cheese.

Clean and cook the spinach in the usual way, and squeeze it very dry. Chop it not too finely, and heat it in a pan with an ounce of butter. Season well. Butter a square cake tin, not too deep. In the bottom put 6 leaves of *fila* pastry cut to the shape of the tin and a fraction larger, brushing the top of each leaf with melted butter before covering it with the next leaf.

Over the 6 layers of pastry spread the prepared spinach, then a layer of the grated Gruyère. Cover with 6 more layers of pastry, again buttering between each layer, and buttering also the top. See that the edges of the pastry are also well buttered, and cook in a moderate oven for 30 to 40 minutes. Leave to cool for a few minutes, turn upside down on to a baking dish, and return to the oven for 10 minutes or so for the underside to get crisp and golden.

Similar dishes are made using for a filling chicken in a *béchamel* sauce (*kotópittá*) or cheese (*tirópittá*).

GRENOUILLES PROVENÇALE

   2 lb frogs' legs (medium size), ½ lb butter, 1 tablespoon olive oil, 1 tablespoon chopped parsley, 2 cloves of garlic (finely chopped), ½ cup milk, ½ cup flour, salt, and ground pepper, juice of ½ lemon, 1 teaspoon chopped chives.

Dip the frogs' legs in milk seasoned with salt and pepper and roll in flour. Heat 2 tablespoons of butter and 1 tablespoon of oil.

Add frogs' legs. Cook until browned, about 12 minutes. Add to them the lemon juice, parsley, chives, and pepper. Keep them warm over a low flame. Now brown the remaining butter until it is the colour of a hazel nut (*beurre noisette*). Add the garlic to the butter and quickly pour it over the frogs' legs. Serve garnished with lemon slices.

BOUDIN PURÉE DE POIS

Take 1½ lb of *boudin* (blood sausage, which in the south of France is always highly seasoned with onions), prick the skin, cut in several pieces and grill them.

For the purée cook ½ lb of dried split peas in water with an onion, a bay leaf, salt and pepper, for 2½ to 3 hours. Put them through a sieve, and if necessary add a little milk and an ounce of butter. Serve piping hot.

TIRI TIGANISMÉNO (Fried Cheese)

Kasséri (hard, salt, goat cheese) is simply cut in squares and fried in very hot oil without benefit of batter or breadcrumbs.

This simple dish can be very good indeed, but it depends very much upon the quality of the cheese. This question of quality applies to all Greek food. Greek gourmets know exactly where the best cheese, olives, oil, oranges, figs, melons, wine, and even water (in a country where water is often scarce, this is not really so surprising) are to be found, and go to immense trouble to procure them.

They are also exceedingly generous and hospitable, and when they see that a foreigner is appreciative, take great pride in seeing that he is entertained to the very best which Greece can offer.

Snails

* *

'I was once present at a learned discussion between two stubborn gentlemen, who were arguing as to the respective merits of the snails of Bourgogne and of those of Provence. They were not speaking of the manner of preparing the snails, but of their natural flavour. One declared that the Bourguignons were more delicate, since they fed on vine-leaves, and the other that those of Provence were more delicious, owing to their diet of thyme and fennel.

'All that is simply absurd. Whatever the snail's food may be, it is improbable, to say the least of it, that any flavour is left after the animal has been starved for thirty or forty days, cleaned in vinegar and salt, rinsed in ten lots of water, and then boiled for several hours.

'Those who succumb (and with reason) to the winy taste of the Bourgogne snails, and those who are enchanted (and one cannot too highly appreciate their attitude) by the thyme and fennel-scented blanquettes of Provence, forget one thing. They forget that the Bourguignon snails have been cooked for an hour in a litre of Chablis, while the Provençals have undergone the same process in salt water, together with a large bunch of thyme and a still larger quantity of fennel. At that rate one might impart the taste of wine or fennel to chewing-gum.

'It is therefore in the manner of preparing them that personal preferences are suited. The choice of snails is of secondary gastronomic importance. For instance, in the case of a dainty dish, the big Bourguignon is preferable to the little grey kind because the shell is thicker and may be left to simmer in its sauce for a long time without danger of cracking.

'Apart from this, it is all a question of personal taste. Both methods of cooking are delicious. These, however, are not the only

44

ways of preparing snails, which you must remember are essential to *aïoli* (garlic and oil sauce).

'It is in the south of France that one finds the most varied snail recipes; there, for instance, they serve them with *sauce piquante*, tomato sauce, and with *sauce verte froide*. At Montpellier, nuts and pounded cracknels are added, together with a great variety of vegetables and herbs chopped fine, such as lettuce, chicory, chervil, celery, marjoram, and basil; elsewhere just a plain vinegar sauce is preferred. In Languedoc, where goose-fat is widely used, snails are prepared with the following sauce:

'You take a fair amount of goose-fat, a large slice of fresh ham cut in dice – the Languedoc housewives affirm that each snail must have its bit of ham – an onion chopped small, and some garlic and parsley also chopped. When this mixture has been browned you add three or four tablespoons of flour and stir briskly until it has turned a golden colour. Sprinkle salt and pepper sparingly before adding the remaining ingredients, which consist of four or five cloves, a little grated nutmeg, some juniper leaves, two sliced lemons, and a generous pinch of saffron. Leave the whole to boil for some minutes.

'Delectable as snails are, people who are lucky enough to live in the country find that the pleasure of eating them is only complete when they have gathered the snails themselves. Few rural delights can compete with that of running through the wet grass, after spring showers, or in the summer after a thunderstorm, in quest of the plump snails. They make their way through shivering grass-blades, or string out across the soft clay like fishing boats leaving port, followed by a silvery wake.

'In catching snails which one will cook oneself, one experiences the joy of the hunter who stalks his prey, anticipating stew, and that of the fisherman casting his line, with *matelote* before his mind's eye.'*

* *The Happy Glutton*, by Alin Laubreaux, translated by Naomi Walford.

GARLIC BUTTER FOR SNAILS (for 50 snails)

> 7 oz butter, 1 or 2 cloves of garlic, a handful of very fresh parsley,
> salt, pepper, pinch of nutmeg.

Chop the parsley very finely indeed. Pound the garlic in a mortar, removing any shreds and leaving only the oil of the garlic. Put the butter into the mortar and work it so that the garlic impregnates it completely, and then add the parsley, which should also be thoroughly worked in and evenly distributed, then add a very little salt, pepper, and nutmeg.

Sometimes a shallot and a few mushrooms, cooked a minute in butter, and chopped with the parsley, are added.

The snails which can be bought in tins, with shells in a separate packet, are quite good. It is really the garlic butter which counts. (Always use this butter when it is absolutely freshly made. The garlic very quickly turns the butter rancid, which is the reason that snails bought ready-filled at *charcuteries* are not always satisfactory.)

To prepare the snails, put one into each shell, and fill it up completely with the prepared butter. The snails are then heated in the oven for a few minutes. On no account must the shells turn over during the cooking or all the butter will run out. The French use special dishes with a little compartment for each snail. Failing these, use little metal or china egg dishes filled with mashed potato in which the shells can be embedded.

The special dishes, the tongs to hold the snails with, and the little forks for extracting them can be bought from Madame Cadec, 27 Greek Street, Soho, W1; and, nowadays, from many other shops catering for the serious amateur cook. Among these are Habitat, 77-9 Fulham Road, SW3; Domus of 109 Clapham High Street, SW4; the kitchen departments of Woollands, Knightsbridge, and Liberty's, Regent Street. Out of London there are Schofield's, Jesus Lane, Cambridge; Brown's of Chester; Harvey's of Guildford; Doodie's Cook Shop at 2 Upper Bow, Lawnmarket, Edinburgh; and Harold Hodgson, Castle Street, Farnham, Surrey.

Fish

Fish

A Venetian Breakfast

* * * * * * * * * * * * * * * * * * * *

'Begin with a Vermouth Amaro in lieu of a cocktail. For hors d'œuvre
have some small crabs cold, mashed up with sauce tartare and a slice or
two of *prosciutto crudo* (raw ham), cut as thin as cigarette paper. After this
a steaming risotto with *scampi* (somewhat resembling gigantic prawns),
some cutlets done in the Bologna style, a thin slice of ham on top and
hot parmesan and grated white truffles and *fegato alla veneziana* complete
the repast except for a slice of *strachino* cheese. A bottle of Val Policella is
exactly suited to this kind of repast and a glass of fine Champagne and of
ruby-coloured Alkermes for the lady, if your wife accompanies you, make
a good ending.

'The Maître d'Hôtel will be interested in you directly he finds that you
know how a man should breakfast.'

The Gourmet's Guide to Europe
by Lt-Col Newnham-Davis and Algernon Bastard, 1903

Shell Fish

* * * * * * * * * * * * * * * * * * *

FRIED SCAMPI

Make a frying batter of 4 oz flour, 3 tablespoons of oil or melted butter, three-quarters of a tumbler of tepid water, a pinch of salt, and the beaten white of an egg. Mix the flour and the butter or oil, adding the water gradually, and keeping the batter smooth and liquid. Make it some time before it is needed, and add the beaten white of egg at the last moment.

Dip the tails of the *scampi*, or Dublin Bay prawns, into the batter and fry them in boiling-hot oil. Nothing else will produce such a crisp and light crust.

Pile the *scampi* up on a dish garnished with parsley and lemon, and, if you like, serve a sauce *tartare* separately, but they are really best quite plain. Whenever possible, make this dish with *scampi* which have not been previously cooked. Simply cut off the head and body of the fish, take the tails out of the shells and dip them raw into the batter.

SCALLOPS *or* COQUILLES SAINT JACQUES

In spite of the instructions given in nearly every cookery book, my own belief is that scallops should not be served in their shells; they tend to dry up when baked in the oven, and however well cooked are inevitably reminiscent of the unpleasant imitations served in bad restaurants – usually flaked cod with a crust of heavy mashed potato.

COQUILLES SAINT JACQUES À LA CRÈME

(sufficient for 2 people)

> 4 scallops, ¼ lb mushrooms, 1 teaspoon tomato purée, 2 egg yolks, 2 tablespoons sherry, 1 large cup cream, 2 oz butter, salt, pepper, lemon juice, parsley, a clove of garlic.

Cut each cleaned scallop in two. Put them in a small pan with the butter, salt and pepper, reserving the red part of the fish. Cook gently for 10 minutes.

At the same time sauté the mushrooms in butter in another pan. Add the sherry, the tomato purée, and the cooked mushrooms to the scallops, then stir in the cream and beaten egg yolks, taking care not to let the mixture boil. Put in the red pieces of the scallops, which will be cooked in 2 minutes, the finely chopped garlic, the parsley, and a little lemon juice.

Serve with triangles of fried bread.

FRIED SCALLOPS À LA PROVENÇALE

Cut the white part of each scallop into two rounds, season with salt, pepper, and lemon juice, dust with flour, and fry them in butter for a few minutes, put in the coral and a little chopped garlic and parsley, and serve with the butter poured over them.

MOULES MARINIÈRE

There are several versions of *moules marinière* Here are three of them.

> 3 quarts mussels, 1 small onion, 1 clove of garlic, 1 small glass white wine, a small piece celery, parsley.

Put the chopped onion, garlic, and celery into a large pan with the white wine and about 1 pint of water. Add pepper but not salt. Put in the well-cleaned mussels, cover the pan and cook until the shells open. Take out the mussels, keep them hot, and thicken the liquid in which they have cooked with 1 oz of butter and ½ oz of flour. Pour the sauce over the mussels in a large tureen and sprinkle with parsley. Serve very hot.

To be eaten out of soup plates, with a fork and a soup spoon.

Another way is to prepare the sauce first; make a little white *roux* in the pan with butter, flour, chopped onion, celery, etc., and the white wine, add the water, and put the mussels in when the liquid has the consistency of a thin soup. The mussels can then be served directly they are opened, a great advantage, as they then do not lose their freshness and savour, which they are apt to do if they are reheated. On no account must the sauce be over-thickened, or you will simply have mussels in a white sauce.

Perhaps the most usual way of cooking *moules marinière* is simply to put the mussels into the pan with the white wine but no water, throw chopped parsley and onion or garlic over them as they are opening and serve as soon as they are all open.

Always serve plenty of French bread with *moules marinière*.

STUFFED MUSSELS

This recipe was given me by a fisherman in Marseille, who made them for me on his boat – and most delicious they were.

For the stuffing: 1 large lettuce, 1 onion, garlic, parsley, 3 oz cooked liver or chopped salame sausage.

Boil the lettuce for 10 minutes, drain well and chop finely with the onion, garlic, parsley, and meat. Open the mussels, which should be the large ones, without separating the two shells. Stuff with a teaspoon of the mixture and tie up each mussel immediately with string. Cook them slowly for 20 minutes in a tomato sauce to which a glass of white wine has been added. Remove the string and serve hot in the sauce.

The above quantity of stuffing is sufficient for 18 large mussels.

MOULES AU CITRON

2 oz carrots, 2 oz butter, ½ oz shallot, 1 tablespoon flour, 4 pints mussels, 2 lemons, bouquet garni, salt and pepper.

Clean the mussels. Chop the carrot and shallot and cook them in a little of the butter, adding salt, pepper, and the herbs. Add the juice of the lemons, then put in the mussels. Cook them rapidly, shaking the pan. As soon as they open, they are cooked. Keep them hot. In another pan put the flour and ½ oz of butter. and when the flour is beginning to turn golden pour on the stock from the mussels, through a fine sieve. Cook another minute or two, finish the sauce with the rest of the butter.

Serve the mussels on the half shells heaped up in a dish, and the sauce separately.

SPAGHETTI WITH MUSSELS

Cook mussels and *clovisses* (small clams)* as for *moules mari-nière*. Shell them and add the liquid to the boiling water in which the spaghetti is to cook. Put in the spaghetti. Add stoned black olives. When the spaghetti is cooked, drain it, heat the mussels 1 minute in the liquid which has come out of their shells, pour on to the spaghetti, sprinkle with chopped parsley, and serve with grated Parmesan cheese.

CRAYFISH WITH SAUCE PROVENÇALE

Make a parsley butter with 2 cloves of garlic pounded, to which you add a ¼ lb of butter and a handful of chopped parsley.

Take 1 lb of crayfish tails out of their shells and put them in a fireproof dish with salt and pepper. Cover them with the parsley butter and place in a hot oven for 10 minutes.

LOBSTER ROMESCO

Prepare the following sauce: grill or roast in the oven 2 tomatoes, a fresh red chilli, several unpeeled cloves of garlic, up to as much as a whole head. Skin the tomatoes and garlic which should be fairly soft by the time it has been roasted a few minutes but must not be charred, and also discard the skin and seeds of the chilli. Pound all ingredients together in a mortar. Add salt and 1 level dessertspoon of paprika (this is a Spanish recipe, and in Spain they use pimentón, which is the Spanish version of paprika). The sauce should be quite thick. Now add 4 or 5 tablespoons olive oil and a little vinegar. Press the sauce through a fine sieve. It should be bright red and quite smooth.

* In England cockles could be used instead.

53

Serve it in a bowl with hot or cold boiled lobster, or with any other fish you please.

ROAST LOBSTERS

This recipe was given in a book of family cookery called *Spons Household Manual*, published in the eighties. It is not intended to be taken seriously, but is given merely as an illustration of the methods, both lavish and somewhat barbaric, of those days.

'Tie a large uncooked lobster to a long skewer, using plenty of pack-thread and attaching it firmly for a reason presently to be stated. Tie the skewer to a spit and put the lobster down to a sharp fire. Baste with champagne, butter, pepper, and salt. After a while the shell of the animal will become tender and will crumble between the fingers. When it comes away from the body the operation of roasting is complete. Take down the lobster, skim the fat from the gravy in the dripping pan, add the juice of a Seville orange, pepper, salt, and spice and serve in a lordly dish.'

RAGOÛT OF SHELL FISH

12 cooked *scampi* or Dublin Bay prawns, 2 quarts mussels, 6 scallops, ¼ lb mushrooms, ½ pint white wine, 1 tablespoon concentrated tomato purée, 1 tablespoon flour, 1 onion, 4 cloves of garlic, seasoning, herbs, 1 dessertspoon sugar, 1 oz butter, parsley.

First of all split the *scampi* tails in half, retaining 6 halves in their shells for the garnish. From the remaining shells remove the flesh and cut it into fairly large pieces.

In a fairly deep pan sauté a sliced onion in butter, when golden add the tomato purée, the chopped garlic, salt, pepper, and the sugar and herbs. Simmer 5 minutes. Stir in the flour. When thick pour over the heated wine, and cook this sauce for 15 to 20 minutes. Add the flesh of the *scampi*, the sliced mushrooms, the scallops cut into two rounds each, and the mussels, which should have been very carefully cleaned. Turn up the flame and cook until the mussels have opened. At the last minute add the reserved *scampi* in their shells. Turn into a tureen or deep dish, squeeze over a little lemon, sprinkle with parsley, and serve very hot, in soup plates.

The black shells of the mussels and the pink of the prawns make a very decorative dish. The tails of large crawfish (*langouste*) can be used instead of the Dublin Bay prawns or *scampi*, but of course fewer will be needed, and they can be cut into four or six pieces each.

Enough for 4 to 6 people as a first course.

Sea and Freshwater Fish

* *

The Fish of the Côte Niçoise

'Nice is not without variety of fish; though they are not counted so good in their kinds as those of the ocean. Soals, and flat-fish in general, are scarce. Here are some mullets, both grey and red. We sometimes see the dory, which is called *Saint-Pierre*; with rock-fish, bonita, and mackerel. The gurnard appears pretty often; and there is plenty of a kind of large whiting, which eats pretty well, but has not the delicacy of that which is caught on our coast. One of the best fish of this country is called *Le Loup*, about two or three pounds in weight; white, firm, and well-flavoured. Another, no-way inferior to it, is the *Moustel*, about the same size; of a dark-grey in colour, and short blunt snout; growing thinner and flatter from the shoulders downwards, so as to resemble an eel at the tail. This cannot be the *mustela* of the antients, which is supposed to be the sea lamprey. Here too are found the *vyvre*, or, as we call it, weaver; remark-able for its long, sharp spines, so dangerous to the fingers of the fisherman. We have abundance of the *saepia*, or cuttle-fish, of which the people in this country make a delicate ragoût; as also of the *polype de mer*, which is an ugly animal, with long feelers, like tails, which they often wind about the legs of the fishermen. They are stewed with onions, and eat something like cow-heel. The market sometimes affords the *écrevisse de mer*, which is a lobster without claws, of a sweetish taste; and there are a few rock oysters, very small and very rank. Sometimes the fishermen find under water, pieces of a very hard cement, like plaister of Paris, which contain a kind of muscle, called *la datte*, from its resemblance to a date. These petrifications are commonly of a triangular form, and may weigh about twelve or fifteen pounds each; and one of them may contain a dozen of these muscles, which have nothing extraordinary in the taste or flavour, though extremely curious, as found alive and juicy in the heart of a rock, almost as hard as marble, without any visible communication with the air or water. I take it for granted, however, that the inclosing cement is porous, and admits the finer parts of the surrounding fluid. In order to reach the muscles, this cement must be broke with large hammers, and it may be truly said, the kernal is not worth the trouble of cracking the shell.* Among the fish of this country there is a very ugly animal of the eel species, which might pass for a serpent; it is of a dusky, black colour, marked with spots of yellow, about eighteen inches, or two feet long. The Italians call it *murena*; but whether it is the fish which had the same name among the antient Romans, I cannot pretend to determine. The antient murena was counted a great delicacy, and was kept in ponds for extraordinary occasions. Julius Caesar borrowed six thousand for one entertainment; but I imagined this was the river lamprey. The murena of this country is in no esteem, and only eaten by the poor people. Crawfish and trout are rarely found in the rivers among the mountains. The sword-fish is much esteemed in Nice, and called *l'empereur*, about six or seven feet long; but I have never seen it.† They are very scarce; and when taken, are generally concealed, because the head belongs to the commandant, who has likewise the privilege of buying the best fish at a very low price. For which reason, the choice pieces are concealed by the fishermen and sent privately to Piedmont or Genoa. But, the chief fisheries on this coast are of the sardines, anchovies, and tunny. These are taken in small

* These are found in great plenty at *Ancona* and other parts of the *Adriatic*, where they go by the name of Bollani, as we are informed by Keysler.

† Since I wrote the above letter, I have eaten several times of this fish, which is as white as the finest veal, and extremely delicate. The emperor associates with the tunny fish and is always taken in their company.

quantities all the year; but spring and summer is the season when they mostly abound. In June and July a fleet of about fifty fishing-boats puts to sea every evening about eight o'clock, and catches anchovies in immense quantities. One small boat sometimes takes in one night twenty-five rup, amounting to six hundred weight; but it must be observed, that the pound here, as well as in other parts of Italy, consists but of twelve ounces. Anchovies, besides their making a considerable article in the commerce of Nice, are a great resource in all families. The noblesse and burgeois sup on sallad and anchovies, which are eaten on all their meagre days. The fishermen and mariners all along this coast have scarce any other food but dry bread, with a few pickled anchovies; and when the fish is eaten, they rub their crusts with the brine. Nothing can be more delicious than fresh anchovies fried in oil; I prefer them to the smelts of the Thames. I need not mention that the sardines and anchovies are caught in nets; salted, barrelled and exported into all the different kingdoms and states of Europe. The sardines, however, are largest and fittest in the month of September. A company of adventurers have farmed the tunny-fishery of the king, for six years; a monopoly, for which they pay about three thousand pounds sterling. They are at a very considerable expense for nets, boats, and attendance. Their nets are disposed in a very curious manner across the small bay of St Hospice, in this neighbourhood, where the fish chiefly resort. They are never removed, except in the winter, and when they want repair; but there are avenues for the fish to enter, and pass, from one inclosure to another. There is a man in a boat, who constantly keeps watch. When he perceives they are fairly entered, he has a method of shutting all the passes, and confining the fish to one apartment of the net, which is lifted up into the boat until the prisoners are taken and secured. The tunny-fish generally runs from fifty to one hundred weight; but some of them are much larger. They are immediately gutted, boiled, and cut in slices. The guts and head afford oil; the slices are partly dried, to be eaten occasionally with oil and vinegar, or barrelled up in oil, to be exported. It is counted a delicacy in Italy and Piedmont, and tastes not unlike sturgeon. The famous pickle of the antients, called *garum*, was made of the gills and blood of the tunny or thynnus. There is a much more considerable fishery of it in Sardinia, where it is said to employ four hundred persons; but this belongs to the duc de St Pierre. In the neighbourhood of Villa Franca, there are people always employed in fishing for coral and sponge, which grow adhering to the rocks under water. Their methods do not savour much of ingenuity. For the coral, they lower down a swab, composed of what is called spunyarn on board our ships of war, hanging in distinct threads, and sunk by means of a great weight, which, striking against the coral in its descent, disengages it from the rocks; and some of the pieces being intangled among the threads of the swab, are brought up with it above water. The sponge is got by means of a cross-stick, fitted with hooks, which being lowered down, fastens upon it, and tears it from the rocks. In some parts of the Adriatic and Archipelago, these substances are gathered by divers, who can remain five minutes below water. But I will not detain you one minute longer; though I must observe, that there is plenty of fine samphire growing along all these rocks, neglected and unknown.'

Travels Through France and Italy
by Tobias Smollet

BOUILLABAISSE

The recipe for Bouillabaisse is already widely known, but as this is a book of Mediterranean cookery it must be included here, and I give the one from M. Reboul's *La Cuisinière Provençale*:

'The serving of Bouillabaisse as it is done at Marseille, under perfect conditions, requires at least seven or eight guests. The reason is this: as the preparation requires a large variety of so-called rock fish, it is as well to make it as lavishly as possible in order to use as many different kinds as are available. Several of these fish have a characteristic taste, a unique perfume. It is upon the combination of all these different tastes that the success of the operation depends. One can, it is true, make a passable Bouillabaisse with three or four kinds of fish, but the truth of the foregoing observation will be generally agreed upon.

'To return to the operation. Having obtained the required fish such as crawfish, *rascasse* (this is a red spiny fish found only in the Mediterranean, it has no English equivalent), gurnet, weever, *roucaou*, John Dory, monk or angler fish, conger eel, whiting, bass, crab, etc., clean and scale them. Cut them in thick slices and put them on two different dishes; one for the firm fish – crawfish,

rascasse, weever, gurnet, angler fish, crab; the other for the soft fish
– bass, *roucaou*, John Dory, whiting.

'Into a saucepan put three sliced onions, four crushed cloves of
garlic, two peeled tomatoes, a branch of thyme, of fennel, and of
parsley, a bay leaf and a piece of orange peel; arrange on the top the
firm fish, pour over them half a glass of oil and well cover it all with
boiling water. Season with salt, pepper, and saffron, and put on to
a very rapid fire. The saucepan should be half in the fire – that is to
say it should be half surrounded by the flames. When it has been
boiling five minutes add the soft fish. Continue boiling rapidly for
another five minutes, making ten minutes from the time it first
came to the boil. Remove from the fire, pour the liquid on slices of
bread half an inch thick arranged on a deep dish. On another
platter arrange the fish. Sprinkle with chopped parsley and serve
both together.

'It should be noted that the cooking is done very quickly, it is
one of the essential factors; in this way the oil amalgamates with the
bouillon and produces a sauce which is perfectly amalgamated,
otherwise it would separate from the liquid and swim on the surface
which is not very appetizing.

'We have rather prolonged this article but this demonstration
was necessary; out of ten cookery books nine will give it incorrectly;
when for example you are told to put all the fish into the pan
together and cook rapidly for 15 minutes, it is impossible that a
piece of John Dory or a slice of whiting which have been boiling
rapidly for a quarter of an hour will still be presentable. Inevitably,
they will be reduced to pulp, this fish being very delicate.

'To make a rich Bouillabaisse one can first prepare a fish *bouillon*
with the heads of the fish which are to go into the Bouillabaisse, a
few small rock fish, two tomatoes, two leeks, and two cloves of
garlic. Strain the *bouillon* and use it for the Bouillabaisse in place of
the water.

'Quite a passable Bouillabaisse can be made with freshwater
fish, such as eels, large perch, medium-sized pike, grayling or trout,
and eel-pout; a dozen prawns can take the place of crawfish. This

will not of course be comparable with the authentic Bouillabaisse of the Mediterranean, but at least it will conjure up memories. . . .'

FISH PLAKÍ

This is a typical Greek way of cooking fish and appears over and over again in different forms.

Wash a large fish, such as bream, chicken turbot, or John Dory. Sprinkle with pepper and salt and lemon juice, and put in a baking dish. Fry some onions, garlic and plenty of parsley in olive oil; when the onions are soft add some peeled tomatoes. Fry gently for a few minutes, add a little water, simmer for a few minutes longer, cover the fish with this mixture, add a glass of white wine, some more sliced tomatoes and thinly sliced lemon. Put in a moderate oven and cook about 45 minutes or longer if the fish is large.

RED MULLET, GRILLED

Grill the cleaned mullets (do not remove the liver) with a little olive oil and serve them with butter into which you have mixed some chopped fennel and a drop of lemon juice.

COLD RED MULLET NIÇOISE

Brown the fish in olive oil; season with salt and pepper and put them in a fireproof dish. Arrange round them some roughly chopped tomatoes, a little minced onion, half a dozen stoned black olives, and a chopped clove of garlic. Pour over half a glass of white wine. Cover the dish and cook in a moderate oven. When they are cold, sprinkle over some parsley and arrange a few slices of oranges along the fish.

MULET AU VIN BLANC

The grey mullet (carefully cleaned) is stuffed with a mixture of fennel, parsley, chopped garlic, and breadcrumbs.

Place it on a bed of sliced onions already melted in olive oil, add a glass of white wine, and cover with breadcrumbs.

Cook in the oven.

BEIGNETS DE SARDINES

Bone some fresh sardines, flatten them out and dip them in frying batter in which you have crushed a small piece of garlic. Fry in hot oil.

MAQUEREAUX AUX PETITS POIS

3 or 4 mackerel, 1 onion, 1 tablespoon olive oil, 1 tablespoon tomato purée, 2 cloves of garlic, bay leaf, fennel, thyme, parsley, 2¼ lb of fresh peas.

Chop the onion finely and sauté it in a braising pan with the olive oil. As soon as it turns golden, add the tomato purée, give it a stir, and put in the garlic and the herbs. Pour over 2½ pints of boiling water, season with salt, pepper, and a pinch of saffron, and put in the peas.

When they are half cooked, add 3 or 4 mackerel cut in 2 or 3 pieces, according to their size. Bring them to the boil, and when the peas and the mackerel are cooked, take out the mackerel and put them on the serving dish.

In another dish arrange some slices of bread, pour over them the peas and the sauce, and serve them all together.

ANGUILLA IN TIELLA AL PISELLI

This is an Italian dish of eel cooked in a frying pan with green peas. Cut the eel into thick slices, and put it into the pan with about ¼ lb of bacon cut into squares, and cook until the eel is lightly browned; then add 1½ lb of shelled green peas, raw, just cover with a thin tomato sauce, season with salt, pepper, and sugar, and simmer until the peas are done.

TRUITE SAUCE AUX NOIX

Put ½ lb of peeled walnuts through a mincing machine, then pound them in the mortar with a little salt, adding gradually a cup of water and a little vinegar, stirring all the time as for a mayonnaise.

Serve the sauce with a cold trout which has been simply poached in a *court bouillon*.

BRANDADE DE MORUE

Another triumph of Provençal cooking, designed to abate the rigours of the Friday fast.

Take some good salt cod, about 2 lb for 6 people, which has been soaked in cold water for 12 hours. Clean it well and put it into a pan of cold water; cover, and as soon as it comes to the boil remove from the fire. Carefully remove all the bones and put the pieces into a pan in which you have already crushed up a clove of garlic and placed over a very low flame. In two other small saucepans have some milk and some olive oil, both keeping warm, but not hot. You now add the oil and the milk alternately to the fish, spoon by spoon, stirring hard the whole time, with a wooden spoon, and crushing the cod against the sides of the pan. (Hence the name *brandade – branler*: to crush or break.) When the whole mixture has attained the appearance of a thick cream the operation is finished; it should be observed however that all three ingredients must be kept merely tepid, or the oil will disintegrate and ruin the whole preparation. Also the stirring and breaking of the cod must be done with considerable energy; some people prefer to pound the cod in a mortar previous to adding the oil and the milk.

Brandade can be served hot or cold, if hot in a *vol au vent* or little pâtés, garnished with a few slices of truffle or simply with triangles of fried bread.

RAÏTO

Raïto is one of the traditional dishes of Christmas Eve in Provence.

It is a ragoût made of onions, tomatoes, garlic, pounded walnuts, thyme, rosemary, fennel, parsley, bay leaves, red wine, capers, and black olives, all simmered in olive oil.

In this sauce either dried salt cod or eels are cooked.

GRILLADE AU FENOUIL

This famous Provençal dish is usually made with a *loup de mer*, a kind of sea bass, one of the best fishes of the Mediterranean. A red mullet can be cooked in the same way. The cleaned fish is scored across twice on each side, salted, and coated with olive oil or melted butter. Lay a bed of dried fennel stalks in the grilling pan, put the fish on the grid, and grill it, turning it over two or three times. When it is cooked put the fennel underneath the fish in a fireproof serving dish; warm some Armagnac or brandy in a ladle, set light to it, and pour it over the fish. The fennel will catch fire, and give off a fine aromatic scent which flavours the fish.

The small amount of sauce which remains after the burning process should be strained before the fish is served. Dried fennel twigs from Provence, as also dried wild thyme on the stalk, and dried whole basil, can be bought from L. Roche, 14 Old Compton Street, London w1.

TUNNY FISH

The consistency of fresh tunny fish is not unlike that of veal. It does not often appear in England, although I have seen it in the shops once or twice. In the south of France it is plentiful and very cheap.

The best way to cook it is to cut it into thick slices, like a salmon steak, and sauté it in oil or butter, adding half-way through the cooking 2 or 3 tomatoes, chopped, a handful of cut parsley, and a small glass of wine, either red or white.

Serve plainly cooked potatoes with it.

BOURRIDE

For anyone who likes garlic this is perhaps the best fish dish of Provence, to my taste much superior to the Bouillabaisse or any of the Italian *zuppe di pesce*.

Bourride is usually made with a variety of large Mediterranean fish, such as *loup de mer* (bass), *daurade* (sea bream), *baudroie* (angler or frog fish), *mulet* (grey mullet), but is successful with almost any white fish, and one variety alone will do. Grey mullet, a despised fish, but very good when properly treated, is excellent for a *bourride*,

FISH

or whiting, rock salmon, gurnard, John Dory, even fresh sardines will do.

Whatever fish is used is poached in a *court bouillon* previously prepared from an onion, bay leaf, lemon peel, fennel, the heads of the fish, salt and pepper all simmered together in water, with the addition of a little white wine or vinegar, for about 15 minutes. Leave this to cool, and strain before putting in the fish and bringing them very gently to the boil, and then just simmering until they are done.

Have ready an *aïoli* (p. 188) made from at least 2 yolks of eggs and about ½ pint of olive oil. Have also ready at least two slices of French bread for each person, either toasted or baked in the oven (the second method is easier to manage, with two or three other operations going on at the same time). When the fish is all but ready put half the prepared *aïoli* into the top half of a double pan; stir into it the beaten yolks of 4 eggs, then a ladleful of the strained *court bouillon* in which the fish are cooking. Cook over very gentle heat, whisking all the time until the sauce is thick and frothy. Pour this sauce over the prepared toast in the heated serving dish, arrange the strained fish on the top, and serve quickly, with the reserved half of the *aïoli* separately.

Octopus and Cuttlefish

* *

A Greek Feast

'. . . We learnt what is meant by a "Feast of the Church".

'The tables were disposed up, across, and down, in the form of a rectangle missing one end. At them sat a company of 60 or 70. In the middle, at the top, presided the bishop who had conducted last night's ceremony, spare and dignified, whose diocese in Asia Minor had been annihilated in the war. By his side was Evlogios, handsomest monk on the Mountain, with his flowing iron beard and broadly chiselled aquiline features. The news had reached us at Vatopedi that he had just been appointed to the archbishopric of Tirana, and would thereby become Primate of Albania, an important post for a man of 47. But he was not certain, he said, whether he wished to exchange the idyll of Athonite existence for the turmoil of that uncouth political fiction.

'The courses began with soup, and continued, four in succession, with octopus. There was octopus cooked amid segments of the garlic bulb, and octopus, more subtly delicate perhaps, alone. There was octopus with beans; and there was octopus again alone but for a hot gravy. Then followed roes, hard and round, an inch in diameter and three long. These were garnished with a yellow mayonnaise of beaten caviare. Their advent was pregnant with event; for, unaware of their resilience, I plunged my knife upon one, to see it fly over my elbow on to the spotless sheen of the father next me. He was ruffled. But, drying the spots with my napkin till they were invisible, I bathed him with such tears of remorse that he was restored to calm. The waiting, directed by Boniface, was faultless. And of the plenty of wine it is unnecessary to speak.

'The climax was reached with snails. These, nine to a dozen on each plate, were served with the tops knocked off. They had to be wheedled therefore, not, as in the West, from the snail's own door, but by an adroit twist of the fork from above. Boniface, all those around us, and even Evlogios from his vantage point, were so concerned lest we should fail fully to appreciate them, that we were at pains to acquire the proper motion. Delicious they were. Meanwhile we drank as though it was ten at night instead of in the morning. All did the same. The conviviality grew. We laughed and shouted and toasted one another across the tables. Then, headed by Evlogios and the bishop, the assembled company took each an empty shell between thumb and forefinger and blew a blast of whistles, as though ten thousand milk boys were competing for a prize.

'Dessert of apples and grapes was succeeded by coffee and the lighter wine. The sun was in the top of the heavens when, having bidden regretful farewell to Boniface, the fierce Epitropos, and all the others, we started out for Caries.'

The Station
by Robert Byron

OCTOPUS

The octopus sounds alarming to those who have not travelled in the Mediterranean; it is in fact an excellent dish when properly prepared, rich and with a reminiscence of lobster.

In Greece and Cyprus the large octopus are dried in the sun; the tentacles are cut into small pieces, grilled over a charcoal fire and served with your apéritif.

To cook them fresh the large ones must be carefully cleaned, the ink bag removed (unless they are to be cooked in their own ink, which makes a rich black sauce, with a very strong flavour), and left in running water for some minutes, then beaten like a steak (in fact I have seen the Greeks bashing them against a rock), for they can be very tough. Then cut off the tentacles and cut the body into strips about the same size. Blanch them in boiling water, drain them and peel off the skin.* The pieces are then put in an earthen-ware casserole with 2 or 3 large onions cut up, garlic, a branch of thyme, salt and pepper, and 2 or 3 tablespoons of tomato pulp, and covered with red wine. Simmer very slowly for 4 or 5 hours.

There are two London fishmongers, Richards, and Hitchcock's, both in Brewer Street, Soho, who sell fresh squid, but although octopus are found in great quantities in northern waters I have never seen them for sale in England, so this recipe can be used equally well for squid or inkfish.

GRILLED CALAMÁRI (cuttlefish, inkfish, squid)

Turn the pocket-like part of the fish inside out, clean under a running tap, remove the ink-bag, the intestines, the hard beak-like protuberance, and the transparent spine bone. Season the fish with salt, pepper, lemon juice, and marjoram, sprinkle with oil and put them under the grill for about 10 or 15 minutes. Served cold and cut into strips crossways these creatures make a good hors d'œuvre.

They can also be stuffed, with spinach or with savoury rice, and cooked *en ragoût*, with a wine or tomato sauce. Cut into fairly large pieces, they are often added to a paëlla or *risotto aux fruits de mer*, and to fish soups.

Very small inkfish, in France *suppions*, in Italy *calamaretti*, in Greece *calamarakia*, are a great delicacy. They are usually dipped in batter, fried crisp in oil, and served with lemon.

CIVET OF INKFISH

3 lb inkfish, 3 lb onions, red wine, pine nuts or almonds.

Clean the inkfish, keep the ink and mix it with a glass of dry red

* A correspondent writing from southern Spain tells me that a more satisfactory way of skinning an octopus is to coat your hand with coarse salt, grab each tentacle hard, and pull. The skin peels off.

wine. Cut the inkfish small, and let them soak overnight in red wine. Next day cut the onions in slices and melt them in a mixture of oil and butter. Take them out, and put in the inkfish and let them take colour. Replace the onions, and a handful of pine-nut kernels or of blanched and split almonds. Add the ink with the wine, and the wine of the marinade. Add water if required. Stew till soft.

Meat

See also chapter on Cold Food.

A Great Restaurant

* * * * * * * * * * * * * * * * * * *

'Vaour is a village I don't know how many miles off Fenayrols. I only know that we went there, and it lies eleven kilometres from a railway station. The Hôtel du Nord at Vaour is illustrious throughout the region for its cookery. People travel vast distances uphill in order to enjoy it. We did. We arrived at eleven o'clock and lunch was just ending. The landlord and landlady in the kitchen said that we were unfortunately too late for a proper meal, but they would see what they could do for us. Here is what they did for us:

Soupe	Perdreau rôti
Jambon du pays	Fromage Roquefort
Confit d'oie	Fromage Cantal
Omelette nature	Confiture de cerises
Civet de lièvre	Poires
Riz de veau blanquette	Figues.

'We ate everything; every dish was really distinguished. I rank this meal with a meal that I once ate at the Étoile restaurant at Brussels, once, if not still, the finest restaurant in the world – and about the size of, say, Gow's in the Strand.

'In addition, there were three wines, a *vin blanc ordinaire*, a *vin rouge ordinaire*, and a fine wine to finish with. The fine wine was fine.

'The total bill, for two persons, was seven francs.'

Things that have Interested Me
by Arnold Bennett

Veal

* * * * * * * * * * * * * * * * * * * *

PAUPIETTES DE VEAU CLÉMENTINE

1 lb lean veal, 1 teaspoonful of capers, juice and peel of half a lemon, ⅛ lb smoked bacon, flour, white wine, herbs, 1 onion, butter.

Have the veal cut in very thin slices. On each small slice of veal squeeze lemon juice and sprinkle pepper and salt. Lay on top of each slice a small piece of smoked bacon. Roll and tie with thread. Roll the paupiettes in flour and fry in butter with the sliced onion, until brown. Add water, a glass of white wine, the lemon peel, capers and herbs, cover the casserole and cook slowly for 45 minutes. Before serving remove the thread from the paupiettes and strain the sauce.

BOCCONCINI

Thin slices of veal (as for escalopes), raw ham, fried bread, Gruyère cheese, egg, and breadcrumbs.

The veal must be cut in very thin, fairly small slices. On each piece of seasoned veal put a piece of raw ham and then a piece of Gruyère cheese. Roll and tie with string. Roll in egg and bread-crumbs, fry in butter until golden. When cooked, the Gruyère cheese should be just melting. Remove the string and serve each one on a slice of fried bread.

NORMAN'S RECIPE

Thin escalopes of veal, raw ham or *prosciutto*, fresh sage leaves, fresh tomato sauce, flour, butter.

On each piece of seasoned veal place a slice of raw ham the same size, and then 1 leaf of sage. Roll and tie with thread. Roll in flour and fry them in butter. Finish cooking them in a well-seasoned tomato sauce (about 15 minutes).

OSSO BUCO

Get the butcher to saw 6 thick pieces of shin of veal, leaving the marrow bone in the centre of the meat. Fry some onions in a wide, shallow braising pan. Pepper and salt the veal, roll in flour and brown in the same pan. Add a carrot, bay leaf, celery, garlic, thyme, basil, and a piece of lemon peel, a glass of white wine, a little stock, and enough freshly made tomato purée to come to the top of the pieces of meat but not to cover them. Cook very slowly for about 4 hours, until the meat is almost coming off the bones. Ten minutes before serving, sprinkle the *osso buco* with finely chopped celery or parsley and lemon peel. Be sure to keep the pieces of meat upright during the cooking, or the marrow in the bones will fall out. Serve a plain risotto as an accompaniment.

CÔTES DE VEAU FOYOT

For 4 good cutlets of veal put about 4 oz of chopped onions into a pan with a little butter and let them cook slowly until they are golden, then add a wineglass of white wine and the same amount of brown stock. Season the cutlets with salt and pepper, roll them in grated Parmesan or Gruyère cheese and then in breadcrumbs. Now butter a fireproof dish, put in a layer of breadcrumbs, then the cutlets, then the onion mixture. Cook uncovered in a very slow oven for about 1 hour, adding a little stock from time to time. Serve with a dish of fresh green peas.

Lamb and Mutton

****

The Ideal Cuisine

' "You are quite right," the Count was saying to Mr Heard. "The ideal cuisine should display an individual character; it should offer a menu judiciously chosen from the kitchen-workshops of the most diverse lands and peoples – a menu reflecting the master's alert and fastidious taste. Is there anything better, for instance, than a genuine Turkish pilaff? The Poles and Spaniards, too, have some notable culinary creations. And if I were able to carry out my ideas on this point I would certainly add to my list a few of those strange Oriental confections which Mr Keith has successfully taught his Italian chef. There is suggestion about them; they conjure up visions of that rich and glowing East which I would give many years of my remaining life to see." '

South Wind
by Norman Douglas

GIGOT À LA PROVENÇALE

A recipe from an old French cookery book which I have left in its original French; as the author rather severely remarks, this dish is supportable only to those who are accustomed to the cooking of the Midi.

76

'On insère symétriquement dans la partie charnue d'un gigot de moyenne grosseur douze gousses d'ail, et deux fois autant de filets d'anchois bien lavés et employés en guise de lardons. Le gigot ainsi préparé est graissé d'huile et cuit à la broche. Tandis que le gigot est à la broche on épluche d'autre part plein un litre de gousses d'ail qu'on fait blanchir dans l'eau bouillante.

'Elles doivent y être plongées à trois reprises différentes, en changeant l'eau à chaque fois, après quoi, on les laisse refroidir dans l'eau froide, et l'on achève leur cuisson dans une tasse de bouillon. Le gigot étant rôti à point, on dégraisse avec soin le jus qu'il a rendu, on en assaisonne les gousses d'ail, et l'on sert le gigot sur cette garniture.

'Ce mets n'est supportable que pour ceux qui sont habitués à la cuisine du Midi, dans laquelle l'ail fait partie obligée de presque tous les mets.'

ARNÍ SOUVLÁKIA (lamb on skewers)

Cut a piece of lamb from the leg into inch cubes. Season with salt, pepper, lemon juice, and marjoram.* Thread the meat on to skewers and grill them. Serve them on a thick bed of parsley or shredded lettuce, on the skewers, with quarters of lemon.

Eaten on the terrace of a primitive Cretan *taverna*, flavoured with wood smoke and the mountain herbs, accompanied by the strong red wine of Crete, these kebabs can be the most poetic of foods. Exquisitely simple, they are in fact of Turkish origin, like many Greek dishes, although the Greeks do not always care to admit it.

MUTTON OR LAMB KEBABS

The unique flavour of these kebabs demands no adornment. They *can* be served on a mound of fried rice, but are best left on the

* In Greece wild marjoram is used; it is called *rígani* and has a much stronger perfume than our marjoram. *Origanum* means in Greek 'the joy of the mountains'. Greek *rígani*, which gives the characteristic aroma and flavour to Greek kebabs, can be bought from the Hellenic Provision Stores, 25 Charlotte Street, London W1.

skewers and laid on a thick bed of parsley or watercress or chopped lettuce.

The lamb or mutton is cut up and seasoned as in the preceding recipe.* Put half a tomato on to each skewer, cut side facing the point. Then thread on alternately the squares of meat with tiny pieces of fat from the meat, bay leaves, and thick slices of onion. Sprinkle with salt, pepper, marjoram (see previous recipe), and lemon juice, and grill them.

For 6 people allow about 3 lb (unboned weight) of leg of lamb or mutton, which should provide 2 full skewers for each person.

LAMB ON THE BONE

In the country districts of Greece, and the islands, the household cooking arrangements are fairly primitive and dishes such as this one are prepared early and sent to the village oven; they emerge deliciously cooked, better than they could ever be in a gas oven, but this method by no means ensures that the food will be served hot. The Greeks in fact prefer their food tepid, and it is useless to argue with them.

Saw a leg of lamb into 4 or 5 pieces, leaving the meat on the bone. Insert a clove of garlic into each piece of meat, season well and sprinkle with rosemary.

Cook in a shallow pan in the oven or over a slow fire, with oil or dripping. About 30 minutes before the meat is done add sliced potatoes and tomatoes. Instead of potatoes, partly cooked rice can be added. In this case, drain off the fat and add plenty of thin tomato purée, which will be absorbed by the rice.

The meat must be very well cooked and almost falling off the bone. Sometimes aubergines cut in half lengthways with the skins left on are added with the potatoes and tomatoes.

* One often sees instructions in cookery books to marinate the meat in wine or vinegar. This is never done in Greece, and would completely ruin the natural beauty of the dish if it were.

TRANCHE DE MOUTON À LA CATALANE

Take a thick slice from a gigot of mutton, put it into a braising pan with a good tablespoon of fat, and fry gently on each side; season with salt and pepper, and place round the meat 20 cloves of garlic* and cook for a few more minutes, sprinkle with flour and pour in a cupful of stock or water and a tablespoon of tomato purée.

Simmer until the meat is cooked, adding more stock if it is getting dry. Serve the meat surrounded by the garlic and with the sauce poured over.

KOKKORÉTSI

The insides of a sheep – heart, liver, lungs, kidneys, brains, sweetbreads, everything – are cut into small pieces, heavily seasoned with mountain herbs and lemon and threaded on to skewers.

The intestines of the animal are cleaned and wound round and round the skewers, which are then grilled very slowly on a spit. They are, in fact, a sort of primitive sausage, the intestine on the outside acting as a sausage skin.

TURKISH STUFFING FOR A WHOLE ROAST SHEEP

> 2 cups partly cooked rice, 1 dozen cooked chestnuts, 1 cup currants, 1 cup shelled pistachio nuts, salt, cayenne pepper, 1 teaspoon ground cinnamon, ¼ lb butter.

Chop the chestnuts and the pistachio nuts finely, mix with the other ingredients. Melt the butter and cook the stuffing in it gently, stirring until all the ingredients are well amalgamated.

This stuffing can also be used for chicken and turkey.

GIGOT DE MOUTON EN CHEVREUIL (leg of mutton to taste like venison)

A medium leg of mutton, choose it short, not freshly killed, and with the fibres close together, and make sure it has no smell of grease.

* The cloves of garlic can be left unpeeled – the skin will come off when they are cooked.

Chop finely a small carrot, a large onion, half a head of celery. Heat in a casserole a wineglass of oil; when it is hot put in the vegetables and brown them lightly. Add ¼ pint of white wine and 2 glasses of wine vinegar. Add 4 or 5 stalks of parsley, 4 large shallots, 2 cloves of garlic, thyme, bay leaf, a good pinch of rosemary, 6 peppercorns, 8 crushed juniper berries, salt. Boil and cook slowly for 30 minutes. Leave to get cold. Remove the skin from the leg of mutton, taking care not to damage the flesh. Lard the surface with 5 or 6 rows of little pieces of bacon, close to each other. Put the leg of mutton into a terrine and pour over the cold marinade. Leave the meat 2 or 3 days in summer, 4 or 5 days in winter. Turn it over with a fork (do not touch with the fingers). Remove any pieces which may be sticking to the meat and wipe thoroughly (important). Put into a roasting dish with melted butter or lard. Start to cook over a very hot fire; this is important, as in a medium oven the meat will boil and not get brown. After it has browned, lower the oven and continue roasting in a good even medium heat and baste frequently.

Serve in a hot dish, surrounded by galettes of pastry and accompanied by a sauce *chevreuil* (see p. 186), and a compote of apples.

FILETS DE MOUTON EN CHEVREUIL (fillets of mutton to taste like venison)

Ask the butcher for 8 small fillets or *noisettes* of mutton, insert small pieces of bacon into each and marinade (see *gigot de mouton en chevreuil*) for 3 days. To cook them, put them in a casserole with butter. When they are cooked, serve with a sauce *poivrade* or any highly seasoned sauce.

SAUCE POIVRADE

Add to the butter in which the fillets have cooked a good pinch of ground black pepper, a small glass of wine vinegar and 2 shallots shredded; reduce this by rapid boiling, and add 2 tablespoons of meat glaze or, failing that, of brown stock, and half a glass of red wine and reduce again.

Beef

****

'Any of us would kill a cow rather than not have beef.'

Dr Johnson

STIPHÁDO (a Greek ragoût)

Cut 2 lb of steak into large pieces. Brown them in oil with 3 lb of small onions and several cloves of garlic. Into the same pan put ½ pint of thick and highly seasoned tomato purée and a glass of red wine. Simmer slowly for 4 or 5 hours, until the meat is very tender and the sauce is reduced almost to the consistency of jam.

BŒUF À L'ITALIENNE

Lard a 3 lb or 4 lb piece of beef with cloves of garlic. Season with salt and pepper, rub with thyme and rosemary and tie up with pieces of fat bacon. Braise in its own fat in a deep braising pan or earthenware dish. Add 2 sliced onions, about ¼ pint of tomato purée, either freshly made, or from 2 tablespoons of concentrated tomato paste thinned with water or stock, 4 whole carrots, 2 whole turnips, a large piece of orange peel, a piece of lemon peel and a glass of Burgundy. Cover the pan and simmer very slowly indeed for

about 8 hours. (The dish can be left in the oven all night at Regulo
1 or 2.)

The sauce will have the consistency almost of jam, the meat
should be so soft it will fall apart at a touch, and the orange and
lemon peel should have dissolved entirely into the sauce.

To serve, cut the carrots and turnips into big strips, sprinkle with
fresh parsley and chopped lemon peel and reheat slowly.

To serve cold remove all fat from the sauce, reheat and then leave
to cool again.

BŒUF EN DAUBE À LA NIÇOISE

3 lb round of beef, 3 cloves of garlic, ¼ lb salt streaky pork or un-
smoked fat bacon, ½ lb carrots, ½ lb stoned black olives, 3 tomatoes,
herbs. For the marinade: ¼ pint of red wine, a coffeecupful of olive
oil, a small piece of celery, a carrot, 4 shallots, an onion, 2 cloves
of garlic, peppercorns, herbs, salt.

Heat the oil in a small pan, put in the sliced onion, shallots,
celery, and carrot. Let them simmer a minute or two, add the red
wine, peppercorns, garlic, and fresh or dried herbs (bay leaf, thyme,
marjoram, or rosemary), and a stalk or two of parsley. Season with a
little salt, and simmer the marinade gently for 15–20 minutes. Let it
cool before pouring over the meat, which should be left to marinate
for at least 12 hours, and should be turned over once or twice.

In an earthenware or other fireproof casserole, into which it will
just about fit, put the meat. Arrange the carrots round it, put in
fresh herbs and the garlic, put the bacon in one piece on top, and
pour over the strained marinade. Cover the pot with greaseproof
paper and the lid, and cook in a slow oven (Regulo 3) for 2½
hours. At this stage add the stoned olives and the skinned and
chopped tomatoes. Cook another half-hour, and before serving cut
the pork or bacon into squares and the meat into good thick slices.

This dish has a really beautiful southern smell and appearance.
Serve with it boiled haricot or flageolet beans, or pasta, or the
aïgroissade toulonnaise (p. 131), and a red Rhône wine.

PEBRONATA DE BŒUF (a Corsican ragoût)

About 2 lb of a cheap cut of beef (top rump, or thick flank, or shin) is cut into dice and browned in olive oil. Add white wine, all kinds of herbs and seasonings, and simmer very slowly.

When it is nearly cooked add the following *pebronata* sauce: a thick tomato purée to which you have added pimentos, onions, garlic, thyme, parsley, pounded juniper berries, and red wine. For the detailed recipe, see p. 190.

FILET DE BŒUF FLAMBÉ À L'AVIGNONNAISE

A small thick fillet for each person, a slice of bread for each fillet, butter, brandy, coarsely ground black pepper, garlic, salt.

Rub the fillets over with garlic and roll them in salt and the black pepper. Put a little butter into a thick pan, make it very hot and put in the fillets and let them sizzle until the outsides are very brown. Add a little more butter, and as soon as it has melted drench the steaks in brandy, set it alight and cook another half-minute after the flames have died down.

In the meantime have ready the slices of bread fried in butter. Slip each one under a fillet, and *serve immediately* with the sauce poured over. The whole process takes about 3 minutes.

CULOTTE DE BŒUF AU FOUR

Cover a 2 lb piece of topside beef with thick pieces of fat bacon, season with salt and herbs and put in a casserole with a glass of white wine. Cover hermetically, seal the lid with flour and water paste and cook in the oven 4 or 5 hours. Serve with the sauce.

FILET DE BŒUF À L'AMIRAL

Slice 5 or 6 onions and fry them in dripping; take them out of the pan and add to them 4 or 5 fillets of anchovies chopped, 2 tablespoons of chopped bacon, pepper, thyme, marjoram, parsley, and 2 yolks of eggs.

Cut a fillet of beef into slices, but not right through, and between each slice put some of the prepared stuffing. Tie the fillet up, put it in a covered pan with dripping, and bake it slowly in the oven.

Pork

****

'Cochon. – C'est le roi des animaux immondes; c'est celui dont l'empire est le plus universel, et les qualités les moins contestées: sans lui point de lard, et par conséquent, point de cuisine, sans lui, point de jambons, point de saucissons, point d'andouilles, point de boudins noirs, et par conséquent point de charcutiers. – Ingrats médecins! vous condamnez le cochon; il est, sous le rapport des indigestions, l'un des plus beaux fleurons de votre couronne. – La cochonnaille est beaucoup meilleure à Lyon et à Troyes que partout ailleurs. – Les cuisses et les épaules de cochon ont fait la fortune de deux villes, Mayence et Bayonne. Tout est bon en lui. – Par quel oubli coupable a-t-on pu faire de son nom une injure grossière!'

Calendrier Gastronomique
by Grimod de la Reynière

RÔTI DE PORC À LA PURÉE DE POMMES

In France a loin or leg of pork is usually sold by the butcher with the rind and some of the fat removed (the French do not set such store by the crackling as we do in England, and the rind is sold separately to enrich stews and soups). This method makes the pork less fat, and also easier to cook. A clove or two of garlic is stuck into the meat, it is seasoned with herbs (marjoram, thyme, or rosemary), and roasted in a rather slow oven. Serve it with a very creamy purée of potatoes, to which should be added, before serving, some of the juice and fat from the roast.

PORK CHOPS MARINATED AND GRILLED

Strew plenty of fresh herbs, such as fennel, parsley, and marjoram or thyme, chopped with a little garlic, over the pork chops. Season with salt and ground black pepper, and pour over them a little olive oil and lemon juice. Leave them to marinate in this mixture for an hour or two. Grill them and serve with a green salad upon which, instead of dressing, you pour the juices and herbs which have fallen from the meat into the grilling pan.

FILET DE PORC AUX POIS NOUVEAUX

For this dish you need a fillet of pork from a young and tender animal. Braise it in a covered pan in bacon fat with onions and a bouquet garni. When it is almost ready, take it out and cut it in slices. Put between each slice a layer of a purée made of fresh green peas which have been cooked with onions and a lettuce heart. Reshape the piece of meat and cover with a well-seasoned *béchamel*. When ready to serve put a beaten white of egg over the whole and sprinkle with breadcrumbs. Place in the oven until it has risen like a soufflé and is golden brown. (Translated from *Plats Nouveaux*, by Paul Reboux.)

FILET DE PORC EN SANGLIER (pork to taste like wild boar)

3½ lb fillet or boned leg of pork. Soak it for 8 days in a marinade of wine vinegar (this is an old recipe from the days when tastes were robust and the powerful taste of a vinegar marinade was liked. Nowadays a marinade of wine, red or white, plus a tablespoon or two of wine vinegar is more suitable) seasoned with salt, pepper, coriander seeds, juniper berries, 2 cloves of garlic, a branch of thyme, a bay leaf, cloves, a branch of basil, a branch of sage, mint, and parsley. Turn the meat each day. Take it out and wipe it. Put it in a very hot oven for the first 15 minutes and leave it to cook 2 hours in a moderate oven. Serve it in a dish surrounded by a purée of chestnuts and accompanied by a sauce *chasseur*.

SAUCE CHASSEUR

Reduce the marinade to one-third of its original quantity. Make a brown roux with 2 oz of butter, 2 oz of flour, and a glass of stock. Add the marinade and finally the gravy from the roast and if possible 2 soupspoons of fresh cream. Serve very hot.

Kid

****

The meat of young kid is much appreciated all over the Mediterranean, especially in the more primitive parts such as Corsica and
the Greek islands. It is hard to say why there is such a prejudice
against this animal in England, and it is only the gastronomically
ignorant who, the moment they go abroad, suppose that whatever
meat they are eating is disguised horse or goat. The textures of these
meats are quite unlike those of veal, beef, or mutton, and there is
besides no call for a French or Italian cook to pretend that he is
serving mutton when it is in fact goat.

In the same way, foreigners in the Middle East are often heard to
complain that they are being served with camel instead of beef. If
they had ever eaten camel meat they would soon know the difference.

Young kid is at its best when roasted on a spit over a wood fire,
and is also cooked *en ragoût* with red wine, tomatoes, and garlic, or
threaded on skewers as for the Greek kebabs, and grilled.

A Corsican way of cooking kid is to stuff a shoulder with a
mixture of chopped veal and pork, the liver of the kid, and spinach,
bound with yolk of egg. The shoulder is roasted and served with
polenta di castagne, a purée of chestnut flour. This chestnut flour is
used in all kinds of ways in Corsica, for cakes, pancakes, soups,
fritters, and sauces.

Boar

* * * * * * * * * * * * * * * * * * * *

Strictly speaking of course boar counts as game, but as it is rare in England I have included it in the meat section, hoping that the recipe might be tried, as Mr Norman Douglas suggests, with a saddle of mutton, with venison perhaps, or even with a leg of pork.

SADDLE OF BOAR

'Trim a saddle of boar and give it a good shape; salt and pepper it, and steep it for 12 to 14 hours in one litre of dry white wine, together with the following seasoning:

> 100 grammes chopped onions
> 100 grammes chopped carrots
> 2 heads of garlic
> 1 head of celery cut in slices
> 1 bay leaf
> 2 cloves
> 10 grammes black pepper
> a pinch of parsley and thyme.

'The saddle should be turned at frequent intervals to absorb the ingredients.

'Now braise it in a stewpan over a slow fire together with the above vegetable seasoning, adding 100 grammes of butter. Baste the saddle with the liquor in which it was lying, and, when this is at an end, with *jus de viande*. The operation should take about two hours, according to the size of the saddle. Then remove from the fire and strain through a sieve the liquor in which it was lying.

'The following hot and thick sauce must meanwhile be held in readiness:

'Put 30 grammes of sugar into a saucepan and melt brown over the fire; then add a claret-glass of wine-vinegar and bring to the boil.

Now add the above strained liquor, together with 25 grammes of roasted pine nuts, 20 grammes each of dried raisins, candied citron peel cut into small squares, and currants (the latter having previously been soaked in water), and 100 grammes of best powdered chocolate. Stir well over the fire. If not sufficiently thick, a little potato flour should be added.

'Serve both as hot as may be. The saddle must be cut in slices immediately, and the sauce poured over the whole. A single non-assertive vegetable, such as purée of chestnuts or lentils – not mashed potatoes: they have no *cachet* – should be served with this, and a rough red wine will be found to marry well with the rather cloying sauce.

' "Not a dish for every day," someone may remark. Assuredly not. The longer one lives, the more one realizes that nothing is a dish for every day. And if anybody will take the trouble to dress a saddle of mutton in the same manner, he will be pleasantly surprised at the result. But I fear we shall go on roasting the beast to the end of time.'*

For the benefit of the adventurous who attempt Mr Norman Douglas's splendid recipe, his measures can be translated approximately as follows:

1¾ pints wine, 3 oz each chopped onion and carrots, ⅛ oz black pepper, 3 oz butter, 1 oz sugar, just under 1 oz roasted pine nuts, ⅔ oz each raisins, candied citron peel, and currants, 3 oz chocolate.

* *Birds and Beasts of the Greek Anthology*, by Norman Douglas.

Substantial Dishes

A Portuguese Supper Party

****

'The play ended, we hastened back to the palace, and traversing a number of dark vestibules and guard-chambers (all of a snore with jaded equeries) were almost blinded with a blaze of light from the room in which supper was served up. There we found in addition to all the Marialvas, the old marquis only excepted, the Camareira-mor, and five or six other hags of supreme quality, feeding like cormorants upon a variety of high-coloured and high-seasoned dishes. I suppose the keen air from the Tagus, which blows right into the palace-windows, operates as a powerful whet, for I never beheld eaters or eateresses, no, not even our old aquaintance Madame la Presidente at Paris, lay about them with greater intrepidity. To be sure, it was a splendid repast, quite a banquet. We had manjar branco and manjar real, and among other good things a certain preparation of rice and chicken which suited me exactly, and no wonder, for this excellent mess had been just tossed up by Donna Isabel de Castro with her own illustrious hands, in a nice little kitchen adjoining the queen's apartment, in which all the utensils are of solid silver.'

The Travel-Diaries of William Beckford of Fonthill
edited by Guy Chapman

RISOTTO WITH MUSHROOMS

This is a very simple form of risotto and, needless to say, all sorts of things can be added – slices of chicken, sautéd chicken livers, beef marrow. It should also be noted that risotto is made with *Italian* rice, which is a round, absorbent variety; no other will serve the purpose so well, the long Patna type of rice being wasted on this dish, for it is not sufficiently absorbent and makes your risotto tough and brittle, whereas a poor quality or small-grained rice will turn into a pudding.

Take 2 cups of Italian rice, 2 pints of chicken stock, 1 medium onion chopped fine, 2 cloves of garlic, 1 wineglass of oil, ¼ lb of white mushrooms cut into slices. Into a heavy sauté pan put the oil and as soon as it is warm put in the onion, the garlic and the mushrooms. As soon as the onion begins to brown, add the rice and stir until it takes on a transparent look. This is the moment to start adding the stock, which should be kept just on the boil by the side of the fire. Pour in about 2 cups at a time, and go on stirring, and adding stock each time it has been absorbed. The whole process is done over a low flame, and in about 45 to 50 minutes, the risotto should be ready. It should be creamy, homogeneous, but on no account reduced to porridge. One must be able to *taste* each grain of rice although it is not separated as in a pilaff. Grated Parmesan cheese is served with it, and sometimes stirred in before bringing the risotto to the table. In any case a risotto must be eaten immediately it is ready, and cannot be kept warm in the oven, steamed over a pan of boiling water, or otherwise kept waiting.

RISOTTO AUX FRUITS DE MER

For 4 people you need:

4 or 5 pints mussels, 1 pint prawns, ½ lb rice, a glass of white wine, 2 shallots or small onions, a clove of garlic, grated cheese, olive oil, black pepper, 2 or 3 tomatoes, and a green or red pimento.

Clean the mussels and put them to cook with 2 pints of water and the white wine, a chopped clove of garlic and shallot, and ground black pepper. When they are open, strain the stock into a basin and leave it while you shell the mussels, and the prawns. Now strain the stock through a muslin, and put it into a pan to heat up. In a heavy pan heat a little olive oil, enough to cover the bottom of the pan, and in it sauté a chopped shallot or onion; add the uncooked rice and stir it round in the oil until it is shiny all over, taking care not to let it stick to the pan; now add a large cupful of the mussel stock, which should be kept simmering on the stove; when the first cupful of stock has been absorbed, add some more; it is not necessary to stir continually, but the pan should be kept on a low flame, and stirred every time more stock is added; as the rice begins to swell and cook, larger quantities of stock can be added and care must be taken that the rice does not stick to the sides of the pan.

In the meantime sauté the tomatoes and the pimento in a little more olive oil, and when the rice is soft add the mussels and the prawns and let them get hot; add this mixture to the risotto only at the last minute, stirring it lightly round. Serve the grated cheese separately, and if you like garnish the dish with a few mussels which have been left in their shells; they make a good decoration.

PAËLLA VALENCIANA (I)

There are countless versions of this celebrated Spanish rice dish. The only constant ingredients in every recipe are rice and saffron; and a mixture of pork, chicken, and shell fish is characteristic, although not invariable. Here is a simple, but authentic, version given me by a Spanish friend.

First, the size and shape of the utensil in which the paëlla is cooked is important. It should be a wide, round shallow pan – and if you are cooking on gas or electricity a heavy one with a flat base – measuring (for the quantities given below, which will make a paëlla for 4 people) approximately 10 to 12 inches in diameter, about 2 inches deep, and with a minimum capacity of 4 pints.

The typical Spanish *paëllera*, which originally gave the dish its name, has two lug or loop handles, depending on whether it is made of earthenware, aluminium, or heavy iron. A large heavy frying pan or sauté pan of approximately the same dimensions also does quite well for the purpose.

Ingredients are:

I small roasting chicken weighing about 1½ lb or half a larger one, about ½ pint of unshelled prawns or 4 oz shelled or 6 giant Mediterranean prawns, 12 French beans (about 2 oz), 2 teacupfuls (10 to 12 oz) of Valencia rice (this is obtainable from Ortega's, the Spanish shop at 74 Old Compton Street, Soho, but Italian Arborio or very good quality Patna rice can be used), 2 tomatoes, and seasonings of saffron, pimentón (this is the Spanish version of paprika pepper, which can be used instead), salt and freshly milled pepper, and olive oil for cooking.

Cut the chicken into about 8 pieces. In the pan warm 4 table-spoons of olive oil. Put in the pieces of chicken, seasoned with salt and pepper. Let them cook very gently for about 12 minutes, mainly on the skin side, as this should be fried to a nice golden colour. Set aside on a plate.

In the same oil fry the peeled and chopped tomatoes; stir in a teaspoon of paprika. Now add 2 pints of water. When it comes to the boil, put back the pieces of chicken and simmer gently for 10 minutes. Add the rice, the prawns (Spanish cooks don't shell them; this is a matter of taste. I prefer them shelled), and the beans topped and tailed and broken into inch lengths. Cook steadily for 15 minutes; sprinkle in half a teaspoon of powdered saffron and a little salt. In another 5 to 7 minutes the rice should be cooked, but timing depends upon the quality of the rice, and the size and thick-ness of the pan and so on. If the water has evaporated before the rice is cooked, add a little more. If on the other hand there is still too much liquid by the time the rice is ready, increase the heat and cook fast until the rice is dry. Finally, taste for seasoning, and serve the paëlla in the pan in which it has cooked.

The rice should be a beautiful yellow colour, and although moist, each grain should be separate. And if it is necessary to stir, use a fork, not a spoon, which might break the rice.

To this basic mixture can be added other ingredients such as small dice of salt pork, mussels, or any other shell fish you please, artichoke hearts, green peas, sweet peppers, sausages, snails, rabbit; and, traditionally, the paëlla is eaten with a spoon although nowa-days forks are more commonly used. Knives should not be required.

In south-eastern Spain, in the regions of Valencia and Alicante, paëlla is the favourite Sunday lunch dish. During the summer, in the country and seaside restaurants which cater for the locals as well as for summer visitors, there is a brisk Sunday trade in paëllas. Late in the afternoon, when the so erroneously named midday meal is at last over, you will see rows of metal paëlla pans, of assorted sizes, all burnished and shining, arranged in serried ranks and left drying in the sun outside the kitchens or in the courtyards.

PAËLLA VALENCIANA (2)

Chicken, lean bacon, oil, garlic, tomato, ground paprika, vegetables, snails, eels, rice, saffron, and crayfish.

Method: First select a medium-sized chicken, cut into 14 or 16 pieces, and salt. Put a decilitre (2½ oz) of good oil into a medium-sized casserole and, when very hot, put the chicken into it and fry lightly, with some pieces of the lean bacon, for five minutes. Then add a small tomato peeled and cut into pieces, a clove of chopped garlic, French beans, and a couple of leaf artichokes (when beans or artichokes cannot be obtained, green peas can be substituted). Then add a teaspoonful of ground red paprika and 400 grammes (about 13 oz) of rice, all well fried, and a litre (all but 2 pints) of hot water. When the water is boiling, add a little saffron, eight small pieces of eel and a dozen snails, and salt to taste.

When the rice is half cooked, add two crayfish per person.

The rice should be cooked on a medium fire. After two or three minutes, cook on a slow heat for another ten or twelve minutes, which is all that is required to have the rice perfect. If you have an oven, it can be put in the oven to dry, but it is more typical to put the casserole on a small fire for a couple of minutes.

If chicken is unobtainable, any kind of game or domestic poultry should be used. But if the flesh is not tender, the paëlla can be cooked as above, except that the rice, previously fried, will not be added until the meat has been cooked for about an hour.

For 4 people.

This recipe came from the Martinez Restaurant in Swallow Street, London, and is reprinted by kind permission of the Wine and Food Society, who originally published it.

ARROZ A LA CATALANA

½ lb rice, 2-3 oz Spanish sausage,* 2 oz fresh pork, 2 oz pork fat, 2 large tomatoes, ½ lb fresh peas, 2 artichokes, 2 sweet red peppers, a squid, a dozen mussels, a few almonds and pine nuts, 2 cloves of garlic, an onion, saffron, parsley.

* Chorizos. These can be bought at Gomez Ortega, 74 Old Compton Street, W1.

Heat the pork fat in a large casserole, and put in the pork and the sausage cut in small pieces, together with the sliced onion. Let them fry a minute or two and add the pimentos, tomatoes, and the squid, all cleaned and cut in slices. Simmer for 15 minutes, add the rice, the peas, the cooked and shelled mussels, the hearts of the artichokes each cut into quarters, the garlic, the almonds and pine nuts, and saffron. Pour over 2 pints of boiling water. Let the whole mixture bubble for a few minutes, then lower the heat and cook gently until the rice is tender. Serve in the pan in which it was cooked, garnished with parsley.

GENOESE RICE

> ½ lb rice, an onion, olive oil or butter, 1 lb of fresh green peas, a few dried mushrooms, ½ lb of coarse country sausage, 2 pints of meat or chicken broth, grated Parmesan cheese.

Chop the onion and put it into a thick pan in which 3 table-spoons of olive oil or 1 oz butter has been heated. When the onion is just slightly golden add the sausage cut into dice, 3 or 4 dried mushrooms, previously soaked ten minutes in warm water, and the shelled peas. Add the heated broth and leave to cook gently while the rice is cooked for 5 minutes in plentiful boiling salted water. Strain the rice, add it to the first mixture, and simmer until most of the liquid is absorbed, but the rice must not be quite dry. Stir in a handful of grated Parmesan, turn the whole mixture into a fairly deep fireproof dish, sprinkle with more cheese and put into a moderate oven for about 20 minutes, until a golden crust has formed on top of the rice.

SULIMAN'S PILAFF (one of the most comforting dishes imaginable)

Into a thick pan put 3 or 4 tablespoons of good dripping or oil, and when it is warm put in 2 cupfuls of rice and stir for a few minutes until the rice takes on a transparent look. Then pour over about 4 pints of boiling water and cook very fast for about 12 minutes. The time of cooking varies according to the rice, but it should be rather under than overdone.

In the meantime, have ready a savoury preparation of small pieces of cooked mutton, fried onions, raisins, currants, garlic, tomatoes, and pine nuts, if you can get them, or roasted almonds, all sautéd in dripping with plenty of seasoning.

Put your strained rice into a thick pan and stir in the meat and onion mixture, add a little more dripping if necessary, and stir for a few minutes over a low flame before serving.

Hand with the pilaff a bowl of sour cream or yoghourt.

To Boil Rice

There are a number of ways of boiling rice and many people have their own pet method. I give here the method I always use and which I have found entirely successful and exceedingly simple.

First: Allow 2 to 3 oz of rice per person. Do not wash it.

Second: Have ready a very large saucepan (not less than 6 pint capacity for 8 oz of rice) full of fast boiling salted water.

Third: Put in the rice, bring the water to the boil again, and let it boil fast for about 15 minutes. The exact time varies with the quality of the rice, the heat of the fire, and so on, and the only way you can be sure it is cooked is to taste it. Strain the rice through a colander, shaking it so that all the water drains out.

Fourth: While the rice is boiling make your oven hot, and have ready a hot dish (preferably a large shallow fireproof platter on which you can serve the rice). When the rice is drained put it on to the hot dish, turn off the oven, and put the rice in it to dry for 3 or 4 minutes. Do not leave the oven on, or the heat will make the grains hard and brittle.

When the rice is to be served plain, a half lemon boiled in the water with it is an improvement.

POLENTA

Polenta is finely ground Indian corn meal; it makes a filling but excellent dish and this is the recipe as it is cooked by northern Italians with large families to feed.

1 lb of polenta will feed 6 hungry people. First prepare a very large heavy pan full of boiling salted water; when the water boils pour in the polenta, little by little, stirring all the time to eliminate lumps and adding more salt and pepper. It will take about 30 minutes to cook, and when ready is the consistency of a thick purée (rather like a purée of dried peas) and is poured out on to a very large wooden board, where it should form a layer about a quarter of an inch thick. Over it is poured a hot and rich tomato or meat sauce (see sauce *bolognese* for spaghetti), which is topped with grated Parmesan cheese. The board is placed in the centre of the table and everybody helps himself. Whatever is left over is trimmed into squares about the size of a piece of toast, and grilled over a very slow charcoal fire; the top crust of sauce and cheese remains undisturbed and the under side, being nearest the heat, is deliciously browned.

To Cook Spaghetti

Buy imported Italian spaghetti.*

Do not break it up unless you want it to turn to a pudding. Allow approximately 2 oz of spaghetti per person; use a very large saucepan, at least 8 pints capacity for half a pound. Have the water well salted and boiling rapidly. The time of cooking varies between 12 and 20 minutes according to the quality of the spaghetti. Have a heated dish, preferably one which will bear a flame underneath, to receive the cooked *pasta*, with a coating of good olive oil on the bottom.

Put the drained spaghetti into this receptacle and stir it round,

* Since this was written the production of spaghetti in England has made great progress, and there is now good English-manufactured spaghetti on the market.

much as you would toss a salad, for a minute or two, so that the whole mass receives a coating of oil and assumes an attractive shiny appearance instead of the porridgy mass too often seen.

Lastly, if you are serving the classic spaghetti *bolognese*, that is, with a thick tomato and mushroom sauce (see p. 184), see that it is highly flavoured, of a suitable thickness and *plentiful*, accompanied by a generous dish of grated cheese.

NEAPOLITAN SPAGHETTI

Neapolitans often like to eat their spaghetti simply with olive oil and garlic; no sauce or cheese.

When the spaghetti is almost ready put several cloves of coarsely chopped garlic with a cupful of the best olive oil into a small pan, and as soon as it is warm pour it over the drained spaghetti in the serving dish and mix it well.

NEAPOLITAN SPAGHETTI WITH FRESH TOMATO SAUCE

This is another favourite Neapolitan way of serving spaghetti. Heat a little olive oil in a frying pan and put in a pound of very red and ripe peeled tomatoes (or the contents of a tin of Italian peeled tomatoes, which make a good substitute). Let them cook a few minutes only, until they are soft but not mushy, add a little chopped garlic, salt and pepper, and a handful of coarsely chopped fresh sweet basil or parsley. Pour the sauce over the spaghetti as soon as it is ready.

SPAGHETTI À LA SICILIENNE

Cook about ¾ lb of spaghetti in the usual way. Meanwhile make ready the following preparation: 4 rashers of bacon cut in large pieces, ¼ lb mushrooms, ½ lb chopped onions, 2 chopped cloves of garlic, a handful of stoned black olives, and 4 anchovy fillets. First fry the onions crisp in fat, add all the other ingredients to the pan, with a handful of coarsely chopped parsley, and cook together for a few minutes. Have ready a hot serving dish into which you put a tablespoon of olive oil, and when the spaghetti is cooked and drained put into the dish, stir round with the oil, pile the onion mixture on to the top in a thick layer and serve very hot, with grated Parmesan handed separately.

NOODLES IN CHICKEN BROTH

Cook the noodles about 8 minutes in the usual way. Drain them well.

Have ready in another pan about 1½ pints of good chicken broth. When it is boiling, put in the noodles and simmer until they are cooked. Stir in then the same mixture as for spaghetti *à la sicilienne* (above) with the oil in which it has been fried.

Serve in soup plates with plenty of broth to each helping, and grated cheese.

FOIE DE VEAU AUX CAROTTES

1½ lb calf's liver, 2 onions, 3 lb carrots, a piece of pig's caul.

Soak the piece of caul in warm salted water for 5 minutes. Slice the liver, season, and tie up in the caul. Fry in butter with the chopped onions. When golden remove from the pan and, with the juice that has come from the liver as a basis, make an *espagnole* sauce (p. 181), but cook only for 20 minutes. Slice the carrots in rounds. Place the *espagnole* sauce in the bottom of a thick pan, put in the carrots and then the liver, still wrapped up in the caul. Cover the pan and cook as slowly as possible for 2½ hours. Before serving unwrap the liver.

Liver cooked in this way also makes an excellent stuffing for tomatoes, aubergines, etc.

CASSOULET TOULOUSAIN

Of all the great dishes which French regional cookery has produced the cassoulet is perhaps the most typical of true country food, the genuine, abundant, earthy, richly flavoured and patiently simmered dish of the ideal farmhouse kitchen. Hidden beneath a layer of creamy, golden-crusted haricot beans in a deep, wide, earthen pot, the cassoulet contains garlicky pork sausages, smoked bacon, salt pork, a wing or leg of preserved goose, perhaps a piece of mutton, or a couple of pig's feet, or half a duck, and some chunks of pork rind. The beans are tender, juicy, moist but not mushy, aromatic smells of garlic and herbs escape from the pot as the cassoulet is brought smoking hot from the oven to the table. French novelists, gourmets, and cooks have devoted pages to praise of the cassoulet, and its fame spread from south-western France, where it originated, first to Paris restaurants, then all over France; recently it has achieved some popularity in this country, no doubt because it seems an attractive solution to the entertaining of a fairly large number of people with little fuss or expense.

A genuine cassoulet is not, however, a cheap dish. Neither are the materials always easy to find. When you consider that in the rich agricultural country of the Languedoc every farmer's wife has the ingredients of the dish within arm's length, festoons of sausages and hams hanging in her kitchen, jars of goose and pork preserved in their own fat on her larder shelves, you understand how the cassoulet came into being; it was evolved to make the best use of the local materials; when you have to go out and buy these things the cost is high (this is just as much the case in France as in England) and although quite a good dish can be made at moderate cost it should be remembered that tinned beans and sausages served in an earthenware casserole do not, alas, constitute a cassoulet.

Bear in mind, also, that a cassoulet is heavy and filling food, and should be kept for cold winter days, preferably for luncheons when none of the party has anything very active to do afterwards.

The ingredients for say 6 people are 1½ lb of good quality medium-sized white haricot beans (butter beans will not do, they are too floury), 1 lb of belly of pork, 1 lb of breast of mutton, ¼ lb of fresh rind of pork, or failing that of ham or bacon, 1 lb of fresh, coarse garlic sausage (not salame, but the kind sold for frying or boiling by French and Continental delicatessen shops), 2 or 3 pieces of preserved goose (in England replace this with half a duck, or omit it altogether), 1 lb of a cheap cut of smoked gammon,

2 or 3 cloves of garlic, herbs, 3 oz of goose dripping or pig's lard, an onion.

Soak the beans overnight. Put them in a large casserole or saucepan, add the onion, garlic, pork rind, the piece of gammon, and a faggot of herbs (bay leaf, thyme, parsley). Cover with fresh water and cook either in a slow oven for 4 to 5 hours or over a direct flame on top of the stove for 1½ to 3 hours (the time of cooking varies a good deal with the quality of the beans). Add salt only in the final stages of cooking.

Meanwhile, roast the pork and the mutton in the dripping (and the duck if you are using this).

When the beans are all but cooked, cut all the meats, the rinds and the sausage into convenient pieces, put them in alternate layers with the beans in a deep earthenware pot and add enough of the liquid in which the beans have cooked to come about half-way up. Put into a fairly slow oven (Regulo 3–4) uncovered, to finish cooking. This final operation can be prolonged to suit yourself by turning the oven right down. Eventually a brown crust forms on top of the beans. Stir this gently into the whole mass, and leave for another crust to form. Again stir it in, and when a third crust has formed the cassoulet should be ready. Sometimes the top is sprinkled with a layer of breadcrumbs when the pot is put in the oven and this speeds up the crusting of the cassoulet, and if perhaps you have added too much liquid the breadcrumbs should help to absorb it. Serve on very hot plates, with plenty of young red wine, and perhaps a green salad and a good cheese to finish the meal.

FOOL *or* EGYPTIAN BROWN BEANS

Fool (brown beans) are the staple food of the Egyptian peasant. 1 lb of these beans and 6 tablespoons of red lentils are washed and put into an earthen or copper casserole with 3 cups of water. This is brought to the boil and then left for hours and hours – all night usually – on a low charcoal fire. If necessary more water can be added. Salt is not put in until the cooking is finished, and olive oil is poured over them in the plate, and sometimes hard-boiled eggs are served with them. The lid of the casserole should be removed as little as possible, or the beans will go black.

The way I cook Egyptian dried brown beans (to be bought nowadays in Soho shops) on a modern cooker is as follows: soak half a pound of them in cold water for about 12 hours. Put them into an earthenware pot well covered with fresh water (about ¾ to 1 pint). Put the covered pot in the lowest possible oven and leave undisturbed all day or all night, or for a minimum of 7 hours. When they are quite soft and most of the water is absorbed, decant them into a shallow serving bowl or dish, season with salt, moisten with plenty of fruity olive oil and lemon juice – or, better still, the juice of fresh limes. Serve separately a plate of hard-boiled eggs. This is a very filling, nourishing, and cheap dish. Tins of ready-cooked Egyptian brown beans are also to be bought in Oriental shops; they are time-saving but still require a good hour of extra cooking, and of course the ritual seasoning of olive oil and lemon.

RAGOÛT DE MOUTON À LA CATALANE

2 lb of leg or loin of mutton, an onion, 2 cloves of garlic, a tablespoon of concentrated tomato purée or ½ lb of fresh tomatoes, ¼ lb of bacon, herbs, ½ lb of chick peas (see p. 132), white wine or port.

Cut the meat and the bacon into thick squares; brown them on each side in pork or bacon fat or oil; add the garlic and the tomato purée or the fresh tomatoes, skinned and chopped, and plenty of thyme or marjoram or basil, and 2 bay leaves. Pour over a glass of sweet white wine, or port. Cover the pan and cook very gently for 2 hours, until the meat is tender.

Have ready the chick peas, soaked and cooked. When the mutton is about ready put the drained chick peas and the meat mixture together into a fireproof dish, put a layer of breadcrumbs on the top and cook in a gentle oven for an hour until a slight crust has formed on the top, and the chick peas are absolutely soft.

Tins of ready-cooked chick peas are now imported from Italy and Egypt. They save much time, but are not as good as those cooked at home. As an emergency store, however, they are useful, especially for dishes such as the above, in which the chick peas are twice cooked and highly seasoned.

Poultry and Game

N.B. – Further recipes for poultry and game will be found in the chapter on Cold Food

Alcobaca

****

'In came the Grand Priors hand in hand, all three together. "To the kitchen," said they in perfect unison, "to the kitchen, and that immediately; you will then judge whether we have been wanting in zeal to regale you."

'Such a summons, so conveyed, was irresistible; the three prelates led the way to, I verily believe, the most distinguished temple of gluttony in all Europe. What Glastonbury may have been in its palmy state, I cannot answer; but my eyes never beheld in any modern convent of France, Italy, or Germany, such an enormous space dedicated to culinary purposes. Through the centre of the immense and nobly-groined hall, not less than sixty feet in diameter, ran a brisk rivulet of the clearest water, flowing through pierced wooden reservoirs, containing every sort and size of the finest river-fish. On one side, loads of game and venison were heaped up; on the other, vegetables and fruit in endless variety. Beyond a long line of stoves extended a row of ovens, and close to them hillocks of wheaten flour whiter than snow, rocks of sugar, jars of the purest oil, and pastry in vast abundance, which a numerous tribe of lay brothers and their attendants were rolling out and puffing up into a hundred different shapes, singing all the while as blithely as larks in a corn-field.

'My servants, and those of their reverend excellencies the two Priors, were standing by in the full glee of witnessing these hospitable preparations, as well pleased, and as much flushed, as if they had been just returned from assisting at the marriage at Cana in Galilee. "There," said the Lord Abbot, "we shall not starve: God's bounties are great, it is fit we should enjoy them." '

The Travel-Diaries of William Beckford of Fonthill

ALEPPO CHICKEN

1 boiling chicken, 1 lemon, carrots, onions, celery, garlic, ½ lb mushrooms, ¼ lb blanched almonds, half a glass of sherry, 4 egg yolks, 1 glass cream.

Rub the chicken over with salt, pepper, and lemon juice, insert a piece of lemon peel in the inside of the bird. Boil with the vegetables in the usual way and when cooked take the pan off the fire, and with a ladle pour out about a pint of the stock into another pan. Add to this the juice of half a lemon, the sherry, the almonds, and the previously sautéd mushrooms, and when hot pour it spoon by spoon on to the eggs beaten up with the cream. Heat gently and when it has thickened put the chicken on a hot dish, and pour the sauce all over and around it.

SHERKASIYA (Circassian Chicken)

1 chicken, 3 oz each of shelled walnuts, almonds and hazel nuts, rice, paprika and cayenne to taste, salt, 2 onions, butter.

Boil the chicken in the usual way, cut it into 4 pieces and arrange it in the centre of a dish of boiled rice.

The following sauce is served with it. Pound the walnuts, almonds, and hazel nuts in a mortar with the paprika and cayenne and salt. Fry the chopped onion in butter and add the pounded nuts and a little of the chicken stock, and when it is thick pour it over the rice.

POLLO IN PADELLA CON PEPERONI

Cut a chicken into 6 pieces. Brown them in a braising pan with olive oil, 2 or 3 onions sliced, 3 cloves of garlic, salt, pepper, marjoram, and thyme; cover the pan and cook slowly for about 1 hour, taking care that the chicken does not burn.

In the meantime put 4 or 5 large red or green pimentos into the oven or under the grill until they are soft and the outer skin can be peeled off; remove the seeds, cut them in strips and add them to the pan with ½ lb of tomatoes roughly chopped and a pinch of basil. When the tomatoes are cooked the dish is ready.

A few slices of orange, peeled and cut in rounds and added at the last moment, are a pleasant addition.

POULET ANTIBOISE

Slice 2 lb of onions and put them into a deep casserole with a half-tumbler of olive oil, a little salt, and a pinch of cayenne pepper.

On top of the onions place a cleaned chicken seasoned with salt and pepper. Cover the casserole and cook very gently in the oven for about an hour and a half. The onions must not brown, but melt gradually almost to a purée, as in *pissaladina* (see p. 39). Add a little more oil during cooking if necessary.

When the chicken is tender carve it into pieces and serve on a dish with the onions all round, garnished with a few stoned black olives and squares of bread, fried in oil.

If the chicken is of the elderly, boiling variety, it can be cut into joints before cooking, so that it will not take so long to cook, although whenever possible I think that chickens should always be cooked whole to preserve the flavour and juices, and carved into joints for serving.

A Delicate Stuffing for Roast Chicken

1 cup cooked rice, a handful raisins, ½ cup blanched and pounded almonds, ¼ cup finely chopped raw onion, ½ cup chopped parsley, liver of chicken, 2 oz butter, a sprig of basil, 1 egg.

Mash the liver and mix all the ingredients together, working the butter well into the mixture, adding the beaten egg last.

ROAST DUCK

The flavour of roast duck is much improved if the cleaned bird is first put into a pan over a hot fire until most of the fat has been extracted. (Watch to see that it does not burn.) Strain the fat off and repeat the process. When all possible fat has been removed put 3 tablespoons of butter into the pan and place it in a hot oven. Baste and turn frequently for 1¼ hours.

OIE RÔTIE À LA BORDELAISE

Another recipe from the same French cookery book as the *gigot de mouton à la provençale*.

Prepare a goose as for roasting; fill the interior with the following stuffing. About 20 fine mushrooms, chopped very finely with the liver of the goose, a pinch of parsley, and a clove of garlic; to this add ½ lb of fresh butter, and ¼ lb of anchovy butter.

Knead all very well together before stuffing the bird; sew up the opening and roast the goose on the spit, exactly as for an unstuffed bird.

Even if the goose is not an excessively fat one, it will still render an abundance of *jus* while it is roasting, owing to the butter in the interior. The bird should be basted almost continuously while it is roasting with this butter, in order that it may be completely pene-trated with the savour of the anchovy butter allied to the garlic. The taste of the goose prepared in this manner is highly esteemed by the gastronomes of the Midi, but apart from the southern *départements*, it is not particularly popular with the majority of gourmets.

LES PERDREAUX AUX RAISINS

In a medium-sized cocotte or braising pan melt a little bacon fat, put in some slices of bacon, a bouquet garni, and two partridges, cleaned and trussed as for roasting. Fill up the pan to the height of the partridges with peeled, somewhat unripe, white grapes. Season with salt and pepper, cover with greaseproof paper and the lid and simmer very gently 1 hour.

Serve very hot with the pieces of bacon and the grapes arranged round the partridges.

AN ITALIAN STUFFING FOR PARTRIDGES

For 4 partridges prepare 4 oz of bacon or ham, ½ lb of mushrooms, and 8 juniper berries, all chopped together with the livers of the birds; wrap the stuffed partridges in bacon and roast, basting with butter.

LES PERDREAUX À LA PROVENÇALE

Another recipe for those who are very fond of garlic.

Into a thick braising pan put a small piece of butter, 2 oz of fat ham or bacon, and 2 cleaned partridges. Fry gently until the partridges are golden, and then add 20 or 30 cloves of garlic chopped with parsley, and fry another 2 or 3 minutes.

Pour over a glass of strong white wine and a glass of thick freshly made tomato purée or a tablespoon of concentrated tomato paste diluted with stock or water. Cover the pan and cook gently for 1½ hours.

Put the sauce through a fine sieve, squeeze in the juice of a lemon and cook another 30 minutes. Use stewing partridges for this dish.

PARTRIDGES COOKED KLEPHTI FASHION

Klephtis (from the word meaning 'to steal') was the name given to the original Greek brigands, who had their headquarters in the mountains of Thessaly and harried the Turks (and anyone else who seemed suitable prey) during their 200 years' occupation of Greece – the original Resistance Movement in fact.

Their method of cooking birds and meat wrapped up in paper in a primitively constructed oven has come to be known all over Greece as 'Klephti cooking'.

The partridges, seasoned with mountain herbs, are wrapped up in paper with a little fat and any vegetables which may be available (in Greece partridges are not treated with the reverence accorded them in England) and placed in an earthen pot, narrowing at the top, called a *stamna*. This pot is then laid on its side in a hollow dug at the edge of a bank of earth, and buried. Underneath the pot the earth is scooped out to make room for a fire of resinous pinewood or charcoal, and this is left slowly burning for 2 or 3 hours.

At any rate, partridges with a piece of fat bacon, wrapped in buttered paper, and cooked in a very slow oven are worth trying. 'Klephti cooking' is always a good way of getting the best flavour out of meat or a bird.

PIGEONS À LA ROMANAISE

Prepare the pigeons as for roasting. Tie each one in a rasher of bacon and a slice of lemon peel. Put them in a shallow pan with 2 oz of butter and sauté them for 10 minutes. Then add a large glass of white wine and the juice of half a lemon and continue cooking slowly until the pigeons are done – about 25 minutes. If the pigeons are of the stewing variety, or the kind sold as rock pigeons, they will need cooking for a good hour, sometimes more. Remove the pigeons from the pan and keep them hot. Strain the liquor from the pan into a double saucepan and stir in 1 oz of butter and the yolks of 2 eggs. Stir continuously as for a sauce *béarnaise*. When it has thickened pour the sauce over the pigeons and serve them with a simplified pilaff of rice (p. 98) containing fried onions and raisins or currants.

PIMENTS FARÇIS DE CAILLES

Bone the quails, 1 for each person. Stuff them with foie gras. Have ready 4 cups of rice cooked as for a pilaff (p. 98). Remove the core and seeds from as many large red pimentos as you have quails. Roll each quail in the rice until it has a coating all round, insert it into the pimento. Put the pimentos into a deep dish with 2 or 3 oz of butter and some tomato sauce to which you have added some brown stock. Cover the dish and braise them on top of the stove for about 30 minutes. They can also be cooked in the oven.

BECFIGUES EN BROCHETTES

The little figpeckers are threaded on skewers, head and all, with the insides left in, about 6 to the skewer, seasoned with pepper and salt and herbs, and grilled.

SNIPE AND MUSHROOMS

In northern Italy this dish is made with little figpeckers and the beautiful wild red mushrooms called *funghi ovali*. In England any small bird, woodcock, snipe, or plover, can be cooked in this way with very excellent results. For each bird you need one very large mushroom; remove the stalks, and lay the mushrooms, stalk side up, in a baking dish. Pour a little oil over them, and place your small bird on the top, seasoned with salt and ground black pepper, put a sprig of fresh thyme or marjoram on top of each bird, and pour over a little more oil. Cover with a greaseproof paper, and cook in a slow oven for about 30 minutes. The mushrooms take the place of the usual croûtons under the bird, and soak up the juices, but the cooking must be gentle, or the mushrooms will shrivel up. For the last 5 minutes of cooking, remove the paper to let the birds brown.

Hare and Rabbit

* *

A Farmhouse Dinner

'Come to Montpazier any time of the year and you will eat well. The thick stone walls are cool in summer and warm in winter, for the wind can whip cruelly about this upland. Then, the low lights of the wood fires seem good after the brilliant grey-green hill-frosts of early winter.

'The food is prepared over a fire in a vast open hearth. The cauldrons, pots and saucepans hang black upon the ratchet. Wood-pigeon and partridge turn on the spits. The dry vine-shoots crisply crackle as the place fills with their blue aromatic smoke and tingling odour.

'This is, indeed, no place to get fussy dishes *à la Cambacérés*,* but go when the game is on and you will eat food for outdoor men and it must be, one likes to think, very like the rustic cooking of the Romans.

'The kitchen is in the hall and you can eat with an eye upon the spits and sizzling pots. That's the way to enjoy a meal, but, luckily, I have run across nowhere in France that peculiarly Iberian combination that used

* *Cambacérés* is one of the signposts, like *parmentier* (potatoes) or *florentine* (spinach). When one reads upon a menu the name of Napoleon's arch-chancellor then look out for something stuffed with foie gras.

not to be rare in Spain: stable, kitchen, bedroom and dining-room all in one – that's very Low Latin indeed.

'Maybe the main dish will be *lièvre à la royale*. There are plenty of thyme and herbs and long runs hereabouts. The hare are tasty.

'Now hare done in Royal Style is a real piece into which go not only your hare and a belly of pork but white wine and meat juice, pears and prunes, garlic, herbs, onions, chestnuts, mushrooms, truffles, red wine, and ham. It's not a city dish. Like all game (and even that glutinous horror, rabbit), the Royal Style is better experienced in the country.

'But before the main dish you will get a fine, thick soup in a deep bowl. Real soup and nothing like the plash of skilly offered us here. None of your timid soup-plates for this juice of the *civet*. If you like a substantial opening to your meal you will, if wise, pour into the soup a quarter of a litre of red wine and drink the whole from the bowl without any new-fangled soup-spoons. This fashion of lapping it up is called by the men of the South-West *faire Chabrol*. No one seems to know why. Perhaps some member of that ancient southern family was a noted *gourmet*.

'Then, depending upon the days, there may be some fish, but we're a good way inland for anything but trout or crayfish. *Écrevisses* can be good enough served in a heaped scarlet *buisson*, a veritable Burning Bush of Crayfish. But such things are, as they say, *pour amuser la gueule* – to amuse the muzzle. We get right down to the *civet à la royale* . . .

'And then come along a brace of *palombes* or wild doves and then the other half of the hare, well grilled . . .

'The sweet-meats, the *entremets*, will be, as always, the weakest part of this rustic meal. Better eat some home-made jam and fresh cream and then tackle the cheeses of the country. Roquefort is their glory and although there are not here such magnificent soft cheeses as Brie and Camembert (at their best) still, the strong and subtle cheeses of the South are worthy of all respect.

'Down here, after all, one is near the Lot and it may well be that the wine is the fruity, purple southern vintage of Cahors, city of Popes and prelates and prunes and memories of pomp. Nearly all the *Coteaux du Lot* are interesting and well sustain the Perigord cooking that ranks with those of Burgundy, Provence, Bresse and Béarn as the best in the French provinces.'

Cross-Channel
by Alan Houghton Brodrick

LIÈVRE À LA ROYALE

This famous recipe for *lièvre à la royale* was invented by Senator Couteaux, who contributed regular articles to the Paris newspaper *Le Temps*. On November 29, 1898, instead of his usual political column, appeared this remarkable recipe. M. Couteaux related at length how he had spent a week in Poitou hunting the right kind of hare; how, the exactly suitable animal at last in his hands, he instantly took the train to Paris, sent out his invitations, and hurried off to consult his friend Spüller, who ran a well-known restaurant in the Rue Favart, to arrange the preparation and cooking of his hare for the following day. The dish takes from noon until 7 o'clock to prepare and cook, and Senator Couteaux tells how by 6 o'clock the exquisite aroma had penetrated the doors of Spüller's restaurant, floated down the street and out into the boulevard, where the passers-by sniffed the scented air; an excitable crowd gathered, and the whole *quartier* was '*mis en émoi*'. If you ever feel like devoting the time (perhaps you need not after all spend a week catching your hare) and the ingredients to cooking this dish you will see that the senator was not exaggerating.

I have translated the recipe as faithfully as possible. It is very lengthy and there are repetitions. But in those days there was plenty of space to fill up; and from the senator's precise instructions one can well imagine the delightful old gentleman bending over his 'daubière', and the pride with which he presented this beautiful creation to his gourmet friends.

'*Ingredients*

'You require a male hare, with red fur, killed if possible in mountainous country; of fine French descent (characterized by the light nervous elegance of head and limbs), weighing from 5 to 6 pounds, that is to say older than a leveret but still adolescent. The important thing is that the hare should have been cleanly killed and so not have lost a drop of blood.

'*The fat to cook it:* 2 or 3 tablespoons of goose fat, ¼ lb of fat bacon rashers; ¼ lb of bacon in one piece.

'*Liquid:* 6 oz of good red wine vinegar. Two bottles of Macon or Médoc, whichever you please, but in any case not less than 2 years old.

'*Utensils:* A *daubière*, or oblong stewing pan, of well-tinned copper, 8 inches high, 15 inches long, 8 inches wide and possessed of a hermetically closing cover; a small bowl in which to preserve the blood of the hare, and later to stir it when it comes to incorporating it in the sauce; a double-handled vegetable chopper; a large shallow serving dish; a sieve; a small wooden pestle.

'*The wine to serve:* Preferably a St Julien or Moulin à Vent.

'*Preliminary Preparations*

'Skin and clean the hare. Keep aside the heart, the liver, and the lungs. Keep aside also and with great care the blood. (It is traditional to add 2 or 3 small glasses of fine old cognac to the blood; but this is not indispensable; M. Couteaux finally decided against this addition.)

'In the usual way prepare a medium-sized carrot, cut into four; 4 medium onions each stuck with a clove; 20 cloves of garlic; 40 cloves of shallot; a bouquet garni, composed of a bay leaf, a sprig of thyme, and some pieces of parsley.

'Get ready some charcoal, in *large pieces*, which you will presently be needing, *burning fast.*

'*First Operation (from half-past twelve until four o' clock)**

'At 12.30 coat the bottom and sides of the stewpan with the goose fat; then at the bottom of the pan arrange a bed of rashers of bacon.

'Cut off the head and neck of the hare: leaving only the back and the legs. Then place the hare at full length on the bed of bacon, on its back. Cover it with another layer of bacon. Now all your bacon rashers are used up.

* These times are given for a dinner to be served at seven o'clock.

'Now add the carrot; the onions; the 20 cloves of garlic; the 40 cloves of shallot;* the bouquet garni.

'Pour over the hare:

(i) the 6 oz of red wine vinegar, and

(ii) a bottle and a half of 2-year-old Macon (or Médoc).

'Season with pepper and salt in reasonable quantity.

'*At one o'clock.* The *daubière* being thus arranged, put on the lid and set the fire going (either a gas stove or an ordinary range). On the top of the lid place 3 or 4 large pieces of charcoal in an incandescent state, *well alight and glowing*.

'Regulate your heat so that the hare may cook for 3 hours, over a gentle and regular fire, continuously.

'*Second Operation (to be carried out during the first cooking of the hare)*

'First chop exceedingly finely the four following ingredients, chopping each one separately:

(i) ¼ lb of bacon.

(ii) the heart, liver, and lungs of the hare,

(iii) 10 cloves of garlic,

(iv) 20 cloves of shallot.

'*The chopping of the garlic and the shallots must be so fine that each of them attain as nearly as possible a molecular state.*

'This is one of the first conditions of success of this marvellous dish, in which the multiple and diverse perfumes and aromas melt into a whole so harmonious that neither one dominates, nor discloses its particular origin, and so arouse some preconceived prejudice, however regrettable.

'The bacon, the insides of the hare, the garlic, and shallots being chopped very fine, and separately, blend them all together thoroughly, so as to obtain an absolutely perfect mixture. Keep this mixture aside.

* In spite of the enormous quantity of garlic and shallots which enter into the composition of *lièvre à la royale*, the remarkable fact is that to a certain extent the two ingredients cancel each other out, so that the uninitiated would hardly suspect their presence.

'*Third Operation* (*from four o'clock until a quarter to seven*)

'*At four o'clock.* Remove the stewpan from the fire. Take the hare out very delicately; put it on a dish. Then remove all the débris of the bacon, carrot, onions, garlic, shallot, which may be clinging to it; return these débris to the pan.

'*The Sauce.* Now take a large deep dish and a sieve. Empty the contents of the pan into the sieve, which you have placed over the dish; with a small wooden pestle pound the contents of the sieve, extracting all the juice, which forms a *coulis* in the dish.

'*Mixing the coulis and the hachis* (*the chopped mixture*). Now comes the moment to make use of the mixture which was the subject of the second operation. Incorporate this into the *coulis*.

'Heat the half bottle of wine left over from the first operation. Pour this hot wine into the mixture of *coulis* and *hachis* and stir the whole well together.

'*At half-past four.* Return to the stewpan:

(i) the mixture of *coulis* and *hachis*,
(ii) the hare, together with any of the bones which may have become detached during the cooking.

'Return the pan to the stove, with the same *gentle and regular fire* underneath and on the top, for another 1½ hours' cooking.

'*At six o'clock.* As the excess of fat, issuing from the necessary quantity of bacon, will prevent you from judging the state of the sauce, you must now proceed to operate a *first removal of the fat.* Your work will not actually be completed until the sauce has become sufficiently amalgamated to attain a consistence approximating to that of a purée of potatoes; not quite, however, for if you tried to make it too thick, you would end by so reducing it that there would not be sufficient to moisten the flesh (by nature dry) of the hare.

'Your hare having therefore had the fat removed, can continue to cook, *still on a very slow fire*, until the moment comes for you to add the blood which you have reserved with the utmost care as has already been instructed.

'*Fourth Operation* (*quarter of an hour before serving*)

'*At quarter to seven.* The amalgamation of the sauce proceeding successfully, a fourth and last operation will finally and rapidly bring it to completion.

'*Addition of the blood to the hare.* With the addition of the blood, not only will you hasten the amalgamation of the sauce but also give it a fine brown colour; the darker it is the more appetizing. This addition of the blood should not be made more than 30 minutes before serving; it must also be preceded by a *second removal of the fat*.

'Therefore, effectively remove the fat; after which, without losing a minute, turn to the operation of adding the blood.

'(i) Whip the blood with a fork, until, if any of it has become curdled, it is smooth again. (Note: the optional addition of the brandy mentioned at the beginning helps to prevent the curdling of the blood.)

'(ii) Pour the blood into the sauce, taking care to stir the contents of the pan from top to bottom and from right to left, so that the blood will penetrate into every corner of the pan.

'Now taste; add pepper and salt *if necessary*. A little later (45 minutes at a maximum) get ready to serve.

'*Arrangements for serving*

'*At seven o'clock.* Remove from the pan your hare, whose volume by this time has naturally somewhat shrunk.

'At any rate, in the centre of the serving dish, place all that still has the consistency of meat, the bones, entirely denuded, and now useless, being thrown away, and now finally around this hare *en compote* pour the admirable sauce which has been so carefully created.'

Needless to say (concludes the senator) that to use a knife to serve the hare would be a sacrilege. A spoon alone is amply sufficient.

CIVET DE LIÈVRE

This Civet consists of the whole hare carefully cut up, with a garnish of cèpes* and croûtons. Do not marinate the hare; in my opinion to do so spoils its fine flavour, and if you have an elderly animal he will do very nicely for a pâté (see p. 144).

In a heavy pan put 4 oz of fat bacon cut in squares, 2 onions finely chopped, 2 or 3 shallots and a clove of garlic, also finely chopped. When they start to turn golden, put in the pieces of hare, which you have carefully wiped. Let them brown on both sides, for about 10 minutes, and then stir in 2 oz of flour, taking care that it does not burn. Add ½ pint of red wine and ½ pint of brown stock. Cover the pan and leave it to simmer for an hour.

Clean and cut in slices ½ lb of cèpes, fry them in oil and add them to the hare (when it has cooked for an hour), and simmer a further 30 minutes. Arrange the pieces of hare in the serving dish and keep them hot. Add to the sauce in the pan the blood of the hare, to which you have mixed a teaspoon each of oil, vinegar, and wine, the pounded liver and a pinch of parsley, thyme, and rosemary.

Reheat the sauce but do not let it boil again, pour it over the hare and garnish with croûtons of fried bread.

LEPRE IN AGRODOLCE

A typical Italian way of cooking game. The chocolate sounds alarming, but serves to sweeten and darken the sauce, and in the blending of the whole the taste of chocolate does not obtrude.

A hare, cut up, vinegar, butter, onion, ham or bacon, sugar, chocolate, almonds, raisins, stock, and seasoning.

Wash the pieces of hare in vinegar, sauté them in butter with the sliced onion, ham or bacon and seasoning, and add the stock.

* Cèpes are not usually obtainable in England, although they do grow in some parts of the country. I have been able to buy them occasionally at Roche's or Parmigiani's, both in Old Compton Street. Dried cèpes are also obtainable in Soho and most delicatessen shops and are worth trying. Soak them for a few minutes and then simmer them in oil until they are tender. They have plenty of flavour. I do not recommend the tinned variety, which are woolly and have no taste whatever. For the *civet de lièvre* cèpes can naturally be replaced with mushrooms, or with chestnuts.

Simmer slowly. Half fill a wineglass with sugar, and add vinegar until the glass is three-quarters full. Mix the vinegar and sugar well together and add to the hare when it is nearly cooked.

Add a dessertspoonful of grated chocolate, a handful of shredded almonds, and stoned raisins, and finish cooking.

LAPIN AU COULIS DE LENTILLES

Cut a rabbit in large pieces, sauté it with bacon and fat. Pour over a glass of white wine or cider, let it bubble a minute or two to reduce, then add seasoning and aromatic herbs. Cover the pan and simmer until the rabbit is tender. Have ready a purée of brown lentils. Mix the liquid from the rabbit into the purée, reduce until thick, add the pieces of rabbit and bacon and reheat.

Vegetables

N.B. – Many of these vegetable dishes constitute a course
in themselves, and are intended to be served as
such, after the meat or fish, when their
full flavour will be appreciated.

The Vegetable Market at Palermo

* *

'The near end of the street was rather dark and had mostly vegetable shops. Abundance of vegetables – piles of white and green fennel, like celery, and great sheaves of young, purplish, sea-dust-coloured artichokes, nodding their buds, piles of big radishes, scarlet and bluey purple, carrots, long strings of dried figs, mountains of big oranges, scarlet large peppers, a last slice of pumpkin, a great mass of colours and vegetable freshnesses. A mountain of black-purple cauliflowers, like niggers' heads, and a mountain of snow-white ones next to them. How the dark, greasy, night-stricken street seems to beam with these vegetables, all this fresh delicate flesh of luminous vegetables piled there in the air, and in the recesses of the windowless little caverns of the shops, and gleaming forth on the dark air, under the lamps.'

Sea and Sardinia
by D. H. Lawrence

POTATO KEPHTÉDÉS (a favourite Greek dish)

Sieve 1 lb cold boiled potatoes, add ½ oz of melted butter, salt, pepper, chopped parsley, a little chopped green onion and 2 finely chopped tomatoes (without the peel), and 2 oz flour. Knead lightly, roll out and shape into rounds. Fry them in a little hot fat or oil, or put them on a greased tin in the oven until golden brown. They should be very soft inside.

POMMES ANNA

A recipe often found in cookery books but less frequently upon the tables of either restaurants or private houses. It is not a southern dish, but makes a very good accompaniment to rich Mediterranean dishes of beef, mutton, hare or other game cooked with wine and herbs. They also make the ideal accompaniment to a Tournedos, or a roast bird of any kind.

For 4 people you need about 1½ lb of potatoes (1 rather large potato per person), an earthenware terrine or metal pan of 1 pint capacity with a close-fitting lid, 3 oz of butter, salt and pepper.

Peel and wash the potatoes. Slice them all the same size, about the thickness of a penny. This is important, in order that they should all be cooked at the same time, and it is laborious to do unless you have a cutter. The perfect instrument is a wooden board with an arrangement of blades. It is called a mandolin. It can be found in the shops which sell imported French kitchen utensils, and is also invaluable for slicing cucumbers thin for salads.

Having sliced your potatoes, wash them well (this does away with any starchy taste) and dry them in a cloth. Coat the inside of your terrine with butter and arrange the potatoes carefully in layers, building up from the bottom and round the sides, so that the slices are evenly distributed, placing small pats of butter and seasoning with a little salt and pepper at intervals. Over the top place a piece of buttered paper and put the cover on.

Cook them in a slow oven (Regulo 2 or 3) for 40 minutes to an hour. They can either be turned out on to a dish or served from the terrine.

It must be admitted that modern English commercially grown potatoes are not very successful for dishes such as *pommes* Anna. Yellow-fleshed, waxy kidney potatoes should be used.

POMMES DE TERRE EN MATELOTE

Cut hot boiled potatoes in half, put them in a casserole with butter, parsley, chives, pepper, and salt, cover with stock or water and a glass of wine. Cook about 10 minutes. Bind the sauce with a yolk of egg.

POMMES DE TERRE À LA MANIÈRE D'APT

Potatoes cut in ¼ inch rounds, 3 tablespoons olive oil, 5 tablespoons fresh tomato purée, salt, pepper, a bay leaf, 6 stoned black olives, breadcrumbs.

Put the olive oil into a shallow gratin dish, add the tomato purée, the potatoes, salt, pepper, and bay leaf, and simmer for 5 minutes.

Barely cover the potatoes with boiling water, and simmer another 30 minutes. Now add the black olives, and cover with a layer of breadcrumbs.

Put in a moderate oven for another 30 minutes.

Serve in the same dish.

SWEET POTATOES (Patátés)

When there was a shortage of potatoes in the Middle East during the war, the Army cooks made the fatal mistake of cooking sweet potatoes like chips, with the result that the whole of the Eighth Army grew to detest these vegetables, and it is true that they are not good when treated as an ordinary potato and served as an adjunct to meat.

They should be baked in their skins, and eaten as a separate course with butter and salt, and they are simply delicious.

The Greeks slice them and make them into sweet fritters, served with a honey sauce.

CAROTTES AU BLANC

Blanch carrots in boiling water, slice them and put them in a casserole with butter, salt, pepper, and parsley. Cover them with milk. When they are cooked bind the sauce with the yolk of an egg.

COURGETTES AUX TOMATES

Slice the courgettes (very young marrows), peeling them only if they are large or blemished. Salt them and leave to stand for 30 minutes. Put them in a fireproof dish with plenty of butter and 2 sliced and peeled tomatoes. Cook for about 10 minutes on a very low flame.

BEIGNETS D'AUBERGINES (I)

In the big markets of Marseille and Toulon there are always one or two stalls selling cooked food, such as *socca* and *panisse* (different sorts of pancakes made of semolina or maize flour), little anchovy pâtés, and these *beignets*, smoking hot from the pan. They are quite excellent.

Without peeling the aubergines, slice them lengthwise very thinly. Salt them and leave them to drain on a plate for an hour.

Squeeze out the water, dip the slices in frying batter (see p. 50) and fry them in very hot oil.

Courgettes can be cooked in the same way.

BEIGNETS D'AUBERGINES (2)

Boil 3 or 4 large aubergines in a little water. When they are soft peel them and put them through a sieve. Add seasoning and cayenne, a little flour to stiffen the mixture and a beaten egg. Shape into rounds, dredge with flour and drop into smoking oil.

AUBERGINES À L'ARMÉNIENNE

Cut the ends of some small aubergines, but leave the skin on. Sauté them in oil, drain them, cut them in half lengthways and take out all the flesh without breaking the skins. Chop the flesh finely and add (for 10 aubergines) about ½ lb of lean minced lamb, 2 tablespoons of finely chopped onion which has been melted a minute or two in oil, 2 tablespoons of chopped pimentos, salt, pepper, 2 or 3 chopped cloves of garlic, a handful of chopped parsley, a handful of little pine nuts, and 2 oz of fresh breadcrumbs.

Fill the aubergines with this mixture, arrange them one against the other in a fireproof dish, sprinkle a little more oil over them, cover the pan and cook them in a gentle oven for 10 minutes.

AUBERGINE DOLMAS (a Turkish and Middle Eastern dish)

8 small round aubergines (or 4 large ones), a cupful of cooked rice, ¼ lb of minced mutton (either raw or cooked), 2 tomatoes, salt, pepper, onions, lemon juice, herbs, a few pine nuts or walnuts, olive oil.

Mix the cooked rice with the well-seasoned meat, a chopped fried onion or two, the chopped tomatoes, and some marjoram, mint, or basil.

Cut about an inch off the thin end of the aubergines, and with a small spoon scoop out most of the flesh. Cut this into dice and mix it with the prepared stuffing. Fill the aubergines with the stuffing (not too full), put the tops in, inverted, so that they fit like corks, lay them in a pan with a little olive oil; let this get hot and then pour hot water over them to come half-way up. Simmer for 30 minutes, add the juice of a lemon, and cook very slowly another 30 minutes. There should be just a very little sauce left by the time they are ready. If there is any stuffing over, use it to fill tomatoes, which can be baked and served with the aubergines.

AÏGROISSADE TOULONNAISE

Make an *aïoli* (see p. 188). Cook a mixture of vegetables – green beans, artichokes, dried haricots, chick peas, etc. Strain them, put in a warmed dish and mix the aïoli into them. Do not reheat.

RATATOUILLE

Ratatouille is a Provençale ragoût of vegetables, usually pimentos, onions, tomatoes, and aubergines, stewed very slowly in oil. This dish has the authentic aromatic flavour of Provençal food.

2 large onions, 2 aubergines, 3 or 4 tomatoes, 2 red or green pimentos,* oil, salt and pepper.

Peel the tomatoes and cut the unpeeled aubergines into squares. Slice the onions and pimentos. Put the onions into a frying pan or sauté pan with plenty of oil, not too hot. When they are getting soft add first the pimentos and aubergines, and, ten minutes later, the tomatoes. The vegetables should not be fried, but stewed in the oil, so simmer in a covered pan for the first 30 minutes, uncovered for the last 10. By this time they should have absorbed most of the oil.

POIREAUX À LA PROVENÇALE

3 lb leeks, ½ lb tomatoes, 1 dozen black olives, 2 tablespoons olive oil, juice of 1 lemon, 1 dessertspoon finely chopped lemon peel.

* See Stuffed Pimentos (p. 136) for the cleaning of pimentos for cooking.

Chop the cleaned leeks into half-inch lengths. Into a shallow heatproof dish put the oil and when it is warm, but not smoking, put in the leeks, add a little salt and pepper, cover the pan and simmer for 10 minutes. Add the tomatoes cut in halves, the stoned olives, the lemon juice and the chopped lemon peel and cook slowly for another 10 minutes. Serve in the dish in which it has been cooked.

This is excellent cold as a salad.

POIS CHICHES (Chick Peas)

These are the *garbanzos* of Spain, where they figure in a great many stews and soups. In Italy they are called *ceci*, and are some-times served mixed with *pasta*. They are also eaten a good deal in the Levant (see the recipe for *hummus bi tahina*, p. 152).

Soak ½ lb of chick peas for 24 hours. Put them in a thick pan and well cover with water. Season with a sliced onion, salt and pepper, sage, and garlic. Put them on the lowest possible flame and while they are cooking do not stir them or let them stop gently boiling or they will never get soft. They will take about 6 hours to cook; an earthenware or enamelled cast-iron pot of chick peas can be left simmering overnight in the slow oven of a solid-fuel cooker.

FENNEL

This is the Florentine, or sweet fennel, much cultivated in southern Europe for its thick and fleshy leaf stalks, as distinct from the common fennel, which will spread like a weed in any English garden, and of which only the delicate little leaves are used in the kitchen.

An absolutely delicious vegetable.

Cut the fennel root-stems, outer leaves discarded, in half and throw them into boiling water. When they are tender (about 20 minutes) arrange them in a buttered fireproof dish, spread grated Parmesan and breadcrumbs on the top and put them in the oven until the cheese has melted.

In the south of France the very young fennel is cut in half and eaten raw, like celery, with salt and lemon juice.

FÈVES AU LARD

Throw young broad beans into boiling water. When cooked, fry some chopped bacon, add a little flour and some of the water in which the beans have cooked. When the sauce has thickened put in the beans, add half a cup of cream. The beans must not cook too long in the sauce or they will lose their fresh flavour.

BROAD BEANS AND ARTICHOKES (a Greek dish)

Cook separately 2 lb of broad beans and 8 artichoke bottoms. Strain the vegetables, keeping a little of the water in which the beans have cooked.

Heat 2 tablespoons of olive oil in a pan, stir in a very little corn-flour, half a cup of the water in which the beans were cooked, the juice of a lemon, some chopped parsley, and add the artichokes and broad beans.

CÉLERI-RAVE FARCI

Celeriac is usually eaten raw. It is peeled, cut into fine strips, and mixed in a bowl with a rather mustardy mayonnaise. But it can be cooked as follows:

Peel 2 or 3 celeriac roots, cut them in half and blanch them.

Prepare the following stuffing: chopped mushrooms and shallots cooked a few moments in butter, to which add a sprinkling of flour, a cup of milk and 2 oz of any minced cold meat or chicken.

Fill the celeriacs with the stuffing (having first scooped out the centres), arrange them in a buttered casserole with more butter on the top, cover the pan and cook them in a slow oven for 45 minutes.

The milk in the stuffing mixture can be replaced by tomato purée.

CAVOLFIORE AL STRACINATI

Cavolfiore is the Italian for cauliflower and *stracinati* means, literally, 'pulled'. Half cook a cauliflower in salted water; drain it, and discard the thick part of the stalk and the leaves, and divide the flowerets. Have ready a pan with warm olive oil in which you have put a clove of garlic chopped, and put in the cauliflower; mash it with a fork and turn it over and over until it is browned on all sides.

ONIONS AGRODOLCE

Put about 25 peeled small onions in a heavy *sauteuse* with 3 tablespoons of olive oil. As soon as the onions start to brown, add a sherry glass of port, one of vinegar, 2 tablespoons of brown sugar, a handful of raisins, salt, and cayenne pepper.

Simmer slowly until the onions are quite soft, and the sauce has turned to a thick syrup.

STUFFED TOMATOES À LA GRECQUE

Displayed in enormous round shallow pans, these tomatoes, together with pimentos and small marrows cooked in the same way, are a feature of every Athenian *taverna*, where one goes into the kitchen and chooses one's meal from the pans arrayed on the stove. It is impossible to describe the effect of the marvellous smells which assail one's nose, and the sight of all those bright-coloured concoctions is overwhelming. Peering into every stewpan, trying a spoonful of this, a morsel of that, it is easy to lose one's head and order a dish of everything on the menu.

Cut off the tops of a dozen large tomatoes, scoop out the flesh and mix it with 2 cups of cooked rice. To this mixture add 2 tablespoons of chopped onion, 2 tablespoons of currants, some chopped garlic, pepper, salt, and, if you have it, some left-over lamb or beef. Stuff the tomatoes with this mixture and bake them in a covered dish in the oven, with olive oil.

TOMATES PROVENÇALES

Cut large ripe tomatoes in half. With a small sharp knife make several incisions crosswise in the pulp of the tomatoes, and in these rub salt, pepper, and crushed garlic. Chop finely a good handful of parsley and spread each half tomato with it, pressing it well in.

Pour a few drops of olive oil on each and cook under the grill for preference, or in a hot oven.

To be quite perfect, *tomates provençales* should be slightly blackened on the cut surface.

TOMATES FROMAGÉES

Choose medium-sized tomatoes, cut off the tops, scoop out the flesh, sprinkle them with salt and leave them to drain.

In a double saucepan melt some Gruyère cheese with black pepper, cayenne, a little French mustard, and a drop of white wine and a pounded clove of garlic.

Fill the tomatoes with the mixture, which should be about the consistency of a welsh rabbit. Bake for 10 minutes in the oven and finish under the grill.

CHAMPIGNONS À LA PROVENÇALE

½ lb fresh field mushrooms, a small glass olive oil, parsley, garlic, salt and pepper.

Wash the mushrooms in cold water; slice them, leaving the stalks on. Heat the oil in a shallow pan, and when it is only fairly hot put in the mushrooms, and sauté them for 5 minutes. Add a handful of chopped parsley, a very little garlic, salt and pepper, and cook 2 or 3 more minutes.

MUSHROOMS À L'ARMÉNIENNE

½ lb mushrooms, 2 rashers bacon, garlic, parsley, olive oil, a glass of wine (red or white).

Slice the mushrooms, sauté them in 2 tablespoons of olive oil; add a few very fine slivers of garlic, and the bacon cut in squares.

Let this cook a few minutes before pouring in a glass of wine, then cook fiercely for just 1 minute (to reduce the wine), turn the flame low and simmer for 5 more minutes.

Mushrooms cooked in this way can be served as a separate course, as a garnish for scrambled eggs or omelettes, added to a *poulet en casserole*, or eaten cold as an hors d'œuvre.

CÈPES À LA BORDELAISE

Wash the cèpes and take the stalks off. If the cèpes are large ones cut them in 2 or 3 pieces. Put a glass of good olive oil in a sauté pan and when it is hot put in the cèpes. Let them brown a little, then turn the fire down very low. In the meantime chop the stalks finely with a handful of parsley and as much garlic as you like. Sauté this mixture in a separate pan, also in oil, then add it to the cèpes. They need about 25 to 30 minutes' cooking.

This method of cooking can be applied to all kinds of mushrooms.

CÈPES À L'ITALIENNE

  1 lb cèpes or morels or other mushrooms, vine leaves, oil, garlic, salt and pepper.

Clean the cèpes, take off the stalks, put them on a dish and sprinkle with salt and leave them a little so that the water comes out of them, then put them in a warm oven a minute or two to dry them.

At the bottom of a fireproof dish lay the washed and dried vine leaves; cover them with a coating of olive oil and put them over the flame until the oil is hot but not boiling; when you put in the cèpes, stalk side up, cover the pan and put in a moderate oven for 30 minutes.

Now cut the stalks into thin pieces, with a clove of garlic, add them to the cèpes, season with black pepper and cook another 10 minutes.

Serve very hot in the dish in which they have cooked.

STUFFED PIMENTOS

No book of Mediterranean cooking would be complete without

this dish, so although it is well known, here is a typical way of doing it.

Cut the stalks off the pimentos and make a small slit down the side of each one, through which you extract the core and the seeds. Take care over this operation and wash the pimentos under the tap, or there will be seeds left in, which are very fiery.

Stuff the pimentos with the same mixture as for tomatoes (p. 134) and put them in a deep baking dish with a moistening of tomato purée and a little oil on the top.

Cover the dish and cook in a medium oven for about 30 minutes.

PIMENTS SAUTÉS

Mixed red, green, and yellow pimentos, cooked a few minutes in boiling water, then peeled and sautéd in butter. The seeds should be taken out before cooking. Especially good as an accompaniment to a veal escalope or cutlet.

TA'AMIA

This Arab way of doing beans makes a delicious *mézé** to serve with drinks.

> 1 cup dried and crushed haricot beans, parsley, green coriander, onion, garlic, salt, teaspoon bicarbonate of soda, handful bread soaked in water.

Wash the beans and soak them overnight. Put all the ingredients through the mincing machine and mix them well. To soften the dough pound it a little in the mortar. Mix in the bicarbonate of soda. Leave the mixture to rest for an hour or two, then cut it into small pieces and fry each one in very hot fat.

FASOŪLIA

The Greek name for haricot beans. People who appreciate the taste of genuine olive oil in their food will like this dish. Soak ½ lb of beans for 12 hours. Heat half a tumbler of olive oil in a deep pan;

* See p. 148.

put in the strained beans; lower the heat; stir the beans and let them simmer gently for 10 minutes, adding 2 cloves of garlic, a bay leaf, a branch of thyme, and a dessertspoonful of tomato paste. Add boiling water to cover the beans by about one inch. Cook them over a moderate fire for 3 hours. The liquid should have reduced sufficiently to form a thickish sauce. Squeeze in the juice of a lemon, add some raw onion cut into rings, some salt and black pepper, and leave them to cool.

Cold Food and Salads

Luncheon at Montegufoni

****

'While we wandered through the high, cool rooms of the great house or, if it were not too hot, along the three sun-baked decks of the garden, Henry would be unpacking an ample luncheon of cold chicken, and Angelo Masti, the peasant in charge, would hurry in with a large, flat, cylindrical cheese, the *pecorino* of the neighbourhood, with a basket of figs and late peaches, tinged with green, and grapes, all still warm from the sun – some of these being of the kind called *fragole*, the small, plump, blue grapes, so different from others in their internal texture, and in their taste, which recalls that of the wood strawberry, that they might be fruit from the planet Mars or Venus – or a huge flask, covered in dry, dusty rushes, of the excellent red wine of the Castle itself. Presently, too, a very strong pungent scent approaching us indicated that Angelo had just bought a large clothful of white truffles from a boy outside, who had been collecting them in the woods. (The white variety is only found, I believe, in Italy, and most commonly in Piedmont and Tuscany, and round Parma: it is coarser than the black, and, in its capacity to impregnate a dish, more resembles garlic, a fine grating of it on the top of any substance being sufficient.) His wife would cook for us, and send in a dish of rice or macaroni sprinkled with them. And these things to eat and drink would be placed on a table covered with the coarse white linen used by the *contadini*, under a ceiling painted with clouds and flying cupids, holding up in roseate air a coat of arms, a crown and a Cardinal's hat.'

Great Morning
by Sir Osbert Sitwell

ASPIC JELLY

For many cold dishes aspic jelly is required as a garnish; the following is a good basic recipe.

Into a large saucepan put a knuckle of veal and a calf's foot, cut in convenient pieces, 2 carrots, 2 leeks (white part only), 1 onion stuck with cloves, the rind of about 6 rashers of bacon, 2 cloves of garlic, a small piece of lemon peel, thyme, bay leaves, and marjoram, salt, a few peppercorns. Should you have the carcass of a chicken, or even the feet and neck, add these as well. Pour a glass of white wine into the pan, then cover the contents with water (about 4 pints for 2½ pints of jelly). Bring the pan to the boil, take off the scum, and then leave to simmer for 4 to 5 hours.

Strain the liquid into a basin and leave it to cool. The next day, when the jelly has set, remove very carefully all the fat, so that no speck remains. To clarify the jelly, put into a saucepan the slightly beaten white of an egg, with the crushed eggshell, a sherry glass of port, a few leaves of tarragon, and a little lemon juice. Add the jelly, bring to the boil, then leave it barely simmering for 15 minutes. Now strain the jelly through a fine cloth, taking care not to stir up the sediment. To obtain an absolutely clear and limpid jelly it may be necessary to put it twice through the cloth.

POULET AUX NOIX

Prepare a concentrated stock by boiling for 2 hours in 1½ pints of water the insides of the chicken with carrots, leeks, turnips, and seasoning. Cut the chicken in pieces, brown in butter; add a few small onions. Cover with the stock, and a spoonful of wine vinegar. Cook for 30 minutes. Meanwhile shell and mince 1 lb of walnuts. From time to time add a little water to thin the oil which comes from the nuts. Add the minced nuts to the chicken and cook another 15 minutes. The sauce should be fairly thick.

Turn into a shallow dish and serve very cold.

COLD CHICKEN VÉRONIQUE

Divide a carefully boiled chicken into several large pieces. Beat up 2 yolks of eggs with ½ pint of cream and a small glass of sherry, and stir over a low flame until it has only slightly thickened. Pour over the chicken. Sprinkle with finely chopped lemon peel and serve very cold. The sauce will thicken when the dish gets cold. This is far superior to the usual chicken salad with mayonnaise. Serve with the following rice salad:

Rice Salad

Boil some rice and while it is still warm mix in some oil, tarragon vinegar, salt, black pepper, and a very little grated nutmeg. Add chopped celery, fresh basil leaves, a few stoned black olives, slices of peeled raw tomato, and red and green pimentos.

LEMON CHICKEN

Poach a chicken with turnips, carrots, onions, and a large piece of lemon peel. Leave the chicken to cool in the stock and when cold take all the meat off the bones and cut into fairly large pieces. Strain the stock, keeping aside the vegetables. Take about 3 large ladles of the stock and heat in a pan. Add 2 tablespoons of chopped lemon rind, the juice of half a lemon and a small glass of sherry or white wine. Simmer 5 minutes, then thicken the sauce with a tablespoon or so of cornflour mixed in a teacup of milk, and when it begins to thicken put in your sliced chicken, the vegetables that were cooked with it cut into long strips and a handful of chopped watercress. Cook all together for a few minutes and turn into a glass dish.

Lemon chicken should be served cold, and the sauce, if made correctly and not too thick, should be very slightly gelatinous and have a translucent appearance. Small chunks of pineapple and a few blanched almonds can be added to this dish.

Note: The vegetables to be boiled with the chicken should be put in whole, otherwise they will be overdone and tasteless.

COLD STUFFED DUCK

If you don't know how to bone a duck probably the butcher or poulterer will do it for you. You must also have ready an aspic jelly made from calf's foot and veal bones, flavoured with garlic and port wine. Stuff the boned duck with a mixture of pâté de foie, plenty of chopped mushrooms and a truffle or two. Sew up the skin, wrap the duck in fat bacon, and roast it for about 25 minutes. Now remove the bacon fat, put the duck into a large shallow terrine, pour the melted jelly all round and place the covered terrine in a larger receptacle containing water, and steam in the oven for about 45 minutes.

Squeeze the juice of an orange over the duck and don't forget to remove the thread; serve cold in its jelly.

PÂTÉ OF CHICKEN LIVERS

Take about 1 lb of chicken livers or mixed chicken, duck, pigeon or any game liver. Clean well and sauté in butter for 3 or 4 minutes. Remove the livers and to the butter in the pan add a small glass of sherry and a small glass of brandy. Mash the livers to a fine paste (they should be pink inside) with plenty of salt, black pepper, a clove of garlic, 2 oz of butter, a pinch of mixed spice, and a pinch of powdered herbs – thyme, basil, and marjoram. Add the liquid from the pan, put the mixture into a small earthenware terrine and place on the ice.

Serve with hot toast.

PÂTÉ DE LIÈVRE

Mince together 2 lb of the raw flesh of a hare with 2 lb of pork and 1 lb of fat bacon, 2 onions, and a little parsley and thyme; add 3 liqueur glasses of brandy, salt and black pepper, and knead them all together until they are well amalgamated. Take one large or several small earthenware terrines, fill them with the mixture, place on top a bay leaf, some bacon rashers cut into thin strips, and a piece of waxed paper. Cover the dishes. Put them in a bain-marie into a slow oven and cook 1 hour for the small terrines, 2 hours for the large. If covered with a thick layer of melted lard, and a piece of wax paper and stored in a cool place, they will keep for months.

This pâté can also be made with rabbit.

TERRINE DE CAMPAGNE

1 lb of belly of pork, 1 lb of lean veal, ¾ lb of bacon, a teacupful of white wine, 2 tablespoons of brandy, a few juniper berries, mace, 2 large cloves of garlic, thyme and marjoram, salt and black pepper, bay leaves.

Remove the rind and any bones from the pork, and cut it, together with the veal (the meat from a knuckle does very well for a terrine) and ½ lb of the bacon, into small squares; if you really have to save time, have the pork and veal coarsely minced by the butcher. Chop the garlic, juniper berries (about 8) and herbs and add to the meat. Season with the ground mace or nutmeg and salt and pepper. Not too much salt, as a good deal is already supplied by the bacon. Put all the meat into a bowl, pour over the white wine and brandy, mix thoroughly, and leave to stand for 2 hours.

Cut the remaining ¼ lb bacon into small strips the length of a match and about ¼ inch wide and thick. Arrange these strips criss-cross fashion at the bottom of the terrine or terrines, and pack in the meat, fairly firmly. Fill almost to the top. Put a bay leaf on the top, and then more strips of the bacon, in the same criss-cross fashion. Stand the terrines in a baking tin half full of water and cook in a slow oven (Regulo 3 or 4) for 1½ hours for small terrines, 2 hours for larger ones. It is the depth of the terrines which is the point to consider. When the terrines have cooled a little, put a piece of greaseproof paper over them and a 2-lb weight on the top and leave several hours. If to be stored, seal with pure pork lard. Should you have the end of a ham to be used up, 1 lb can be used instead of the ½ lb of bacon, but be very sparing with salt.

JAMBON PERSILLÉ DE BOURGOGNE

This is the traditional Easter dish of Burgundy. The recipe comes from the famous Restaurant des Trois Faisans at Dijon.

Soak a ham for 24 hours, in order to desalt it. Half cook the ham in a large pan of unsalted water reckoning 10 minutes to the lb instead of the usual 20. Drain it, remove the rind, and bone and divide it into large pieces.

Put it to cook again with a knuckle of veal of about 1 lb in weight cut in pieces; 2 calf's feet, boned; a bouquet garni of chervil and tarragon; 10 white peppercorns tied in a muslin, a little salt, and cover it with a white Burgundy. Bring it to the boil, and then continue cooking gently, on a steady heat, so as to preserve the limpidity of the stock, which is to become the jelly; skim off the fat which rises to the surface from time to time.

When the ham is cooked, and *very* cooked, mash it a little with a fork, and turn it into a large bowl, pressing it down with a fork. Strain the liquid through a muslin, add a little tarragon vinegar. When the liquid has started to jelly, stir in 2 tablespoons of chopped parsley. Pour this jelly over the ham, and keep it in a cold place until the next day.

OIE EN DAUBE

Put the goose into a thick fireproof casserole with diced bacon, parsley, shallots, garlic, thyme, bay leaf, basil, 2 glasses of water, 2 of red wine, ½ glass of cognac, salt and pepper. Hermetically seal the pan and cook very slowly for 5 hours. Strain the sauce and when it is cool remove the fat, pour back over the goose and serve cold. Chicken can be cooked the same way, either whole or cut into joints.

BŒUF À LA MODE À LA PROVENÇALE

3 or 4 lb of round or topside of beef. Lard the meat with small pieces of bacon and cloves of garlic. Tie round with string, season with salt and pepper and brown on all sides in bacon fat. Put into a deep casserole, cover with a quantity of well-fried onions, 5 or 6 carrots, a piece of celery, a piece of orange or lemon peel, thyme, bay leaf, peppercorns, cloves, and a calf's foot cut up, cover with half water and half red wine. Cook extremely slowly either on top of the stove or in the oven (Regulo 1 or 2) for 7 or 8 hours.

Remove the meat, which should be so soft it can be cut with a spoon, take off the string and put it into the serving dish. Strain the sauce over, and, when it is cold, remove the fat. The meat should be entirely covered with a soft clear jelly.

Serve with potatoes baked in their jackets and a plain salad, but no other vegetables.

FILET DE PORC FRAIS TRUFFÉ FROID

This beautiful recipe is given by Paul Poiret in his *107 Recettes et Curiosités Culinaires*.

'You need a fine fillet of pork, cut from a young animal; cut some uncooked *truffes* in pieces about the size of a pigeon's egg. With the point of a knife make a number of deep incisions, a few centimetres apart, in the inside of the filet. Into each incision introduce a piece of *truffe*, pushing it well in towards the centre of the fillet, to produce a marbled effect. When the fillet is thus piquéd with the *truffes*, season it with salt and pepper, roll it up into a good shape, tie it with string, and roast it.

'Leave it to cool in its own fat, and serve it cold the next day.'

PICTÍ

Pictí is the Greek brawn.

A pig's head is boiled for hours in water strongly flavoured with bay leaves and peppercorns.

When cooked it is cut up into chunks, the juice of 3 or 4 lemons is added to the strained stock, which is poured over the brawn, arranged in large earthenware basins, and left to set.

Not very elegant, but usually very good.

CHANFAÏNA OF LIVER (a Spanish dish)

1 lb pig's liver, 3 tablespoons olive oil, 4 onions, a few mint leaves, 2 or 3 parsley stalks (finely chopped), 2 red pimentos, 3 cloves, a pinch of cumin, a pinch of cinnamon, a pinch of saffron, black pepper, breadcrumbs.

Blanch the liver, cut in pieces, in salted water. In the oil put all the other ingredients, except the breadcrumbs.

Cook them a minute or two, and add the strained liver, and a little of the water it has been cooked in, let it simmer a few minutes, then stir in the breadcrumbs.

Pour the whole mixture into a dish and serve cold.

PIMENTOS TO SERVE WITH COLD MEAT

(Escoffier's recipe.)

Warm half a wineglass of olive oil in a thick pan. Put in 1 lb of finely chopped white onions and 2¼ lb of pimentos, from which you have removed the core and the seeds; cut in rounds. Cover the pan and let them simmer 15 minutes, when you add 2 lb of very ripe peeled tomatoes, a clove of garlic, a teaspoon of powdered ginger, 1 lb of sugar, ½ lb of sultanas, and a teaspoon of mixed spice. Pour over a pint of good vinegar and continue cooking very slowly for 3 hours.

Note on Hors d'Œuvre

As I have not given a separate chapter for hors d'œuvre I have included a few in this section on cold food. In Spain, the south of France, and Italy an hors d'œuvre is a very simple affair, consisting usually of olives, salame sausage, a tomato or pimento salad, and a few anchovies in oil, or alternatively a plate of fresh shell fish, prawns, or *oursins* (those spiny sea-urchins cut in half from which you scoop out the coral with a piece of bread). The Genoese are fond of an antipasto of *sardo* (a hard ewe's milk cheese imported from Sardinia), young raw broad beans, and the local, rather highly flavoured salame. In Greece your *mézé* (the equivalent of our hors d'œuvre) is eaten while you drink your apéritif and not as part of the main meal. You can sit at a table on the sand with your feet almost in the Aegean as you drink your *oúzo*; boys with baskets of little clams or *kidónia* (sea quinces) pass up and down the beach and open them for you at your table; or the waiter will bring you large trays of olives, of which there are dozens of different kinds and colours in Greece, the most delicious being the purple Calamata olives in oil, dishes of *atherinous* (tiny fried fish rather like our whitebait), slices of fresh crumbly cheese called *mysíthra*, or *graviera* (the Cretan Gruyère), small pieces of grilled octopus, minute *kephtédés* (little rissoles made of crushed haricot beans and fried in oil), quarters of fresh raw turnip (this sounds doubtful but is in fact delicious for there is no vegetable more vegetable-tasting than these little turnips freshly dug up from the garden), slices of fresh cucumber cooled in ice water; all this accompanied by limes or lemons and a mound of bread. There are also many kinds of smoked or cured fish – *lakerda* (a kind of smoked tunny fish), red caviar or *brique*, *botargue* (pressed tunny fish eggs made into a kind of sausage and eaten in slices with oil and lemon), and *taramá* for which I have given a recipe.

In Turkey and Egypt there is a kind of ham called *bastourma*, of Armenian origin, heavily spiced with garlic and red pepper, and in the Greek islands the peasants make a small fillet of ham called *louza* strongly flavoured with herbs, which is excellent. The Cypriots have little sausages heavily spiced with coriander seeds, and the Italians dozens of different local salame and country hams, best of which are the *prosciutto di San Daniele* and *prosciutto di Parma* (raw Parma ham) which, eaten with fresh figs, or melon, or simply with butter, must be the most perfect hors d'œuvre ever invented.

BLACK OLIVES

'The whole Mediterranean, the sculpture, the palms, the gold beads, the bearded heroes, the wine, the ideas, the ships, the moonlight, the winged gorgons, the bronze men, the philosophers – all of it seems to rise in the sour, pungent taste of these black olives between the teeth. A taste older than meat, older than wine. A taste as old as cold water.'*

GREEN OLIVES

Olives to serve with cocktails or as hors d'œuvre are better bought by the pound, not in bottles; prepare them in this way, as they do in Marseille.

Choose the small, oblong French or Greek olives. In each olive make an incision with a knife, and put them in layers in a jar with some pieces of cut garlic and 2 or 3 stalks of thyme, and a small piece of chilli pepper, fill the jars up with olive oil, and cover them. In this way they can be stored for months.

* *Prospero's Cell*, by Lawrence Durrell.

Black olives can be treated in the same way, or simply put straight into olive oil without the garlic or thyme. Cyprus green olives are cracked and spiced with coriander.

AMBELOPOÙLIA

These are the tiny birds called *beccafica* or figpeckers. In Cyprus they are preserved in vinegar and eaten whole, bones and all.

Pluck a dozen *beccafica*, cut off the feet, and, if they are to be preserved, the heads as well, but do not clean them out.

Bring a small saucepan of water to the boil, add a teaspoon of salt and boil the little birds in this for 5 or 6 minutes. Take them out of the water, drain them well, and allow them to cool. They can then be eaten cold as they are, or preserved for as long as a year by being put into a glass or earthenware jar and covered with wine vinegar, to which a tablespoon of salt is added or not, as you please.

DOLMÁDES

Dolmádes, little rolls of savoury rice in vine leaves, are a favourite first course in Greece, Turkey, and the Near East. Sometimes meat, pine nuts, and even currants are mixed with the rice. Here is the basic version:

For 3 dozen vine leaves you need about 2 teacups of cooked rice mixed with enough olive oil to make it moist, a little chopped fried onion, and a flavouring of allspice and dried mint. Blanch the vine leaves in boiling salted water. Drain them. Lay them flat on a board, outer side downwards. On the inside of each leaf lay a teaspoon of the rice, and then roll the leaf tucking in the ends as for a little parcel and squeeze this roll in the palm of your hand; in this manner the *dolmádes* will stay rolled up and need not be tied. When they are all ready put them carefully in a shallow pan, squeeze over plenty of lemon juice and add about a cup (enough to come half-way up the pile of *dolmádes*) of tomato juice or good stock. Cover with a small plate or saucer resting on top of the *dolmádes* and fitting *inside* the pan. The plate prevents the *dolmádes* moving during the cooking. Keep them just simmering for about 30 minutes. They are best eaten cold.

Excellent stuffed vine leaves imported in tins from Greece are now available in many supermarkets and delicatessen shops. Simply turn them out of the tin, rinse them in a colander, arrange them in a pyramid on a flat dish, and squeeze lemon over them.

SALAD OF AUBERGINES

A good dish from Greece and the Near East, where it is often served as a *mézé*. You dip slices of bread into the salad and eat it while drinking your apéritif.

Grill 3 or 4 large aubergines in their skins. When they are soft, peel them and pound the flesh in a mortar with 2 cloves of garlic, salt and pepper. Add, drop by drop, a little olive oil, as for a mayonnaise. When it is a thick purée, add the juice of half a lemon and a handful of chopped parsley.

The grilling of the aubergines gives the finished dish a characteristic slightly smoky flavour. If preferred they can be boiled or baked instead of grilled.

AUBERGINES IN A MARINADE

Cut the aubergines in half, lengthways, without peeling them. Sprinkle them with salt and leave them for 2 hours. Drain off the water which has come out of them, and fry them lightly in oil.

Then put them in jars, and pour over them a marinade consisting of 2 parts oil to 1 part white wine, or wine vinegar.

They will keep like this for some days, and are served as hors d'œuvre, or can be stuffed or used in a stew.

TARAMÁ AND TARAMÁSALATA

Taramá is the name given to dried, salted, pressed, and slightly smoked cod's roe, sold out of a barrel – a favourite *mézé* in Greece and Turkey. Genuine Greek *taramá* can be bought from King Bomba's Italian Produce Stores, 37 Old Compton Street, London WI.

Take about ¼ lb of *taramá* and pound it in a mortar with a clove or two of garlic, lemon juice, and about 4 tablespoons each of olive oil and cold water, added alternately and very slowly, until the preparation has the consistency of a thick and smooth purée. *Taramásalata* is served with bread or hot toast.

The taste of Greek *taramá* is not unlike that of the more heavily smoked but less salt English cod's roe, which can be treated in the same way, the skin having first been removed (or one can use cod's roe paste from a jar). Sometimes a slice or two of white bread, crusts removed, softened in cold water and then squeezed dry, is added to the cod's roe during the mixing process. It helps to diminish the saltiness of the fish, gives a milder taste and a thicker consistency.

SARDINES MARINÉES À LA NIÇOISE

Fresh sardines are grilled and then put to marinate for a few days in olive oil, with a drop of vinegar, a bay leaf, peppercorns and herbs, and served as hors d'œuvre.

HUMMUS BI TAHINA

An Arab dish. *Tahina* is the sesame paste which is to be found in Oriental stores* in London, and which is mixed with oil and garlic and thinned with water to make a sauce which in Arab countries is eaten as a salad, with bread dipped into it.

For this hors d'œuvre the ingredients are ½ lb of chick peas, a cupful each of *tahina*, olive oil, and water; a little lemon juice, mint, and garlic.

Cook the previously soaked chick peas in plenty of water, slowly, for about 6 hours. They should be very soft for this dish. Strain them, pound them to a fine paste, or if you prefer, put them through the food mill. Pound two or three cloves of garlic into the purée, stir in the *tahina*, the olive oil, the lemon juice, and season

* The Hellenic Provision Stores, 25 Charlotte Street, John and Pascalis, 35 Grafton Way, Tottenham Court Road, The Little Pulteney Stores, Brewer Street, WI.

with salt and pepper. Add water until the mixture is about the consistency of a thick mayonnaise. Stir in about 2 tablespoons of dried or fresh mint. The mixture is poured either into a large shallow dish, or on to saucers, one for each person, and sets fairly firmly when cold.

TAHINA SALAD

Pound a clove of garlic in a mortar; stir in a cupful of the *tahina* paste, salt, pepper, half a cupful of olive oil, half a cupful of water, lemon juice, and coarsely chopped parsley. The *tahina* should be of the consistency of cream. In Egypt and Syria a bowl of *tahina* is served either with pre-lunch drinks or as an hors d'œuvre, with pickled cucumbers, pickled turnips, and the flat round bread (Esh Baladi) of the country. The *tahina* is eaten by dipping the bread into the bowl.

PAN BAGNIA (a Provençal sandwich)

Cut fresh French rolls in half lengthways. Rub them with garlic. Spread with stoned black olives, pieces of red or green sweet pepper, tomato, and young raw broad beans. Pour a little olive oil and vinegar over the rolls, join the two halves together and put them under a heavy weight for 30 minutes.

Pan bagnia is served in Provençal cafés with a bottle of wine when a game of *boules* is in progress. The ingredients vary according to what is in season, or what is available. There may be anchovies, gherkins, artichoke hearts, lettuce. Probably it is the origin of *salade niçoise* which is made with the same variety of ingredients, but without the bread.

TIAN

'One of the national dishes of Provence, but a family dish; one that the tourist will search for in vain on the menus of restaurants.

'It is the container which indicates the contents, and the *tian* owes its name to the vast and heavy terrine of the earthenware of

Vallauris, where it is sent to cook on a wood fire in the baker's oven. The dish consists of a gratin of green vegetables, spinach, and chard (*blettes*), sometimes mixed with marrows, all finely chopped, and first melted in – this is essential – olive oil. For this reason the dish is to be found in olive-growing areas. But from one region to another the dish is subject to all kinds of variations, which give it its local *cachet*. Up in the hills they do not despise the addition of salt cod, on the coast this is replaced with fresh sardines or anchovies.

'This savoury mosaic can also be enriched with a few cloves of garlic, a cupful of rice, or a handful of chick peas. Another refinement is to thicken it with eggs and cover the top with breadcrumbs and Parmesan.

'*Tian* is one of those ready-made dishes which is eaten cold on picnics. There is a story that six gourmets from Carpentras, having decided to treat each other, each provided at the time fixed for the picnic a surprise dish of a monumental *tian*; all six were devoured with patriotic enthusiasm. Not one of the guests had been able to imagine that there was a better dish in the world.'

From *La Cuisine à Nice*, H. Heyraud

PATAFLA (a good recipe for a cocktail party or a picnic)

4 tomatoes, 1 large onion, 2 green pimentos, 2 oz black olives, 3 oz green olives, 2 oz capers, 2 oz gherkins, 1 long French loaf.

Peel the tomatoes, stone the olives, take the core and seeds out of the pimentos, and chop them together with all the other ingredients. Cut the loaf in half longways, and with a sharp knife remove all the crumb, which you mix with the tomato preparation, kneading it all together with a little olive oil, a pinch of paprika, black pepper and salt.

Now fill the two halves of the loaf with the mixture, press them together and put the loaf into the refrigerator.

To serve, cut into slices about a quarter-inch thick, and pile them up on a plate.

Always make *patafla* the day before it is needed.

COLD FOOD AND SALADS

A PROVENÇAL SALAD

Mix shredded celery with chopped watercress, grated orange peel, parsley, garlic, stoned black olives, and slices of tomato. Oil and lemon dressing.

OIGNONS À LA MONÉGASQUE

Choose small pickling onions. Peel them and put them into a little boiling water.

When they are half cooked add olive oil, a little vinegar, 2 or 3 chopped tomatoes, thyme, parsley, a bay leaf, and a handful of currants. They are served cold.

SALAD OF SWEET PEPPERS

Cold cooked red peppers (or mixed green and red) with oil and vinegar dressing.

LEEKS À LA GRECQUE

Boil some small leeks. When they are nearly cold drain most of the water away, leaving enough to cover them. Stir some of this water into a teaspoon of cornflour, add to the leeks and stir until the sauce thickens a little. Squeeze in the juice of a lemon, stirring all the time, and add a tablespoon of olive oil. Let the leeks get cold in the sauce, which should be slightly gelatinous and shiny.

Serve as it is.

SALADE DE HARICOTS BLANCS SECS

Cold boiled haricot beans, drained and mixed while still warm with oil and vinegar, chopped raw onions, slices of salame sausage, and parsley.

SALADE AUX ÉPINARDS

Plunge some cleaned spinach into boiling water for 3 minutes. Drain it, mix with some sliced cold potatoes and thin slices of Gruyère cheese. Dress with a spoonful of cream and the juice of a lemon.

PICKLED CUCUMBER SALAD

Into a bowl of yoghourt mix a little of the vinegar from pickled cucumbers, a handful of chopped mint, and a little sugar. Into this mixture put the sliced pickled cucumbers.

A Few Sweets

A Few Sweets

Ices in Athens

****

'Somewhere round about half-past six that evening I was taken to a famous café at the end of the university boulevard, the name of which eludes my memory. Here faced by the prospect of nothing but boiled rice for days to come I was presented by the waiter with a card on which some thirty different kinds of ices were listed. The temptation was atrocious. My soul responds to a mere vanilla ice smeared out into the thick glass of an Italian ice-cream vendor; but here was an opportunity to sample ices which were to the ordinary vanilla as Hyperion to a satyr. Although I knew nothing could be worse for my complaint than even a moderate indulgence in ices, greed and curiosity were too much for me. I really did feel that life was less important than sampling these ices to discover which were the most delicious. Some of the fervour which has given martyrs to science was mine. I understood and sympathized with the impulse that drives a man to explore the North Pole. I comprehended at last the passionate recklessness of Bluebeard's Fatima. Even without dysentery and cystitis it would have been impossible for any man to sample every ice on that list, and I do not remember that ever in my life I was so anxious to make a right choice. Paris faced by the problem of awarding an apple to the most beautiful of three goddesses was in no predicament at all compared with mine. I looked at the waiter. Could I rely on his taste to direct me aright, so that whatever pain I might suffer on the morrow would not be embittered by the thought that for all I was suffering I had chosen the wrong ices? And while I was trying to decide with what varieties I should make myself that amount more ill than I was already I found myself being introduced to the wives of various members of the British Naval Mission whose habit it was to meet here at dusk. . . . I heard which were the best six ices on the list and of those six I ate four. Then, thinking of that boiled rice before me and deciding that I might as well make the most of what life remained to me, I wound up my last night of freedom with a mayonnaise of crayfish at dinner.'

First Athenian Memories
by Compton Mackenzie

I have included only a few sweets in this collection. The sweet course in these southern countries, and particularly in the eastern Mediterranean, frequently consists of very sweet little cakes and pastries, and bowls of fresh fruit. The cakes usually require quantities of eggs, sugar, honey, almonds, pistachio nuts, rose-water, sesame seeds, and other Arabian Night ingredients. Very often little bowls of yoghourt are handed round and eaten with sugar and a conserve of quinces or little oranges, more like jam than our compote.* The Greeks are also much addicted to a slab-like cold rice sweet, called *rizogalo*, liberally sprinkled with cinnamon, *loukoumadés*, which are like very small doughnuts served in a honey syrup, and *baklawá*, the honey and almond cakes which originated in Turkey.

The huge selection of ices which had such allure for Mr Compton Mackenzie are still, so far as I know, a speciality of the large cafés in Athens; one does not find them, though, in the small *tavernas* and typical Greek restaurants. The Athenians dine very late, so they sit in these cafés drinking *oúzo* or Varvaresso brandy until nine o'clock in the evening. After dinner they will return to the café to eat ices and sweet cakes with their Turkish coffee.

In the summer fresh fruit is put on the table in bowls of ice, melon is served at the end of a meal, not at the beginning, and the beautiful *pastèque*, or water melon, is much eaten for its thirst-quenching properties.

In the winter there are the succulent dried figs and raisins of Greece and Smyrna; tender little apricots dried with their stones in from Damascus, and *loucoumi*† to accompany sweet Turkish coffee.

In Italy there will be delicious water ices (*granite*), Sicilian *cassata*, and elaborate ice-creams (although both of these are eaten as refreshments at odd times of the day more than at the end of a meal; they have also become rather Americanized in recent years).

---

* In Greece these conserves are always offered to a stranger arriving at the house, served on a tray with a glass of water and a small cup of sweet Turkish coffee, a symbol of hospitality which must on no account be refused.

† Turkish Delight.

A FEW SWEETS

The Neapolitans make very beautiful-looking fan-shaped pastries, filled with cream cheese and spices, called *sfogliatelle*, and their Christmas sweet, *pastiera napoletana*, is a rich and solid confection of eggs, butter, sugar, almonds, spices, and crushed wheat.

The Spaniards may offer nougats, *turrons* (delicious almond or marzipan confections), or quince or peach paste as sweetmeats. In Spain, too, I have enjoyed delicate sponge cakes and very light sweet biscuits for breakfast. The little town of Apt, in the Comtat Venaissin, in northern Provence, produces delicious candied apricots and other *fruits confits*, and no one who has seen them will forget the gorgeous displays of crystallized fruits of every conceivable variety in the shops of Nice, Cannes, and Genoa.

In the rose-coloured city of Toulouse there is scarcely a street without a confectioner's window showing little boxes of candied violets, and one of the best of all French sweetmeats are the delicate, diamond-shaped little almond paste *calissons* of Aix-en-Provence.

Nearly all these delicacies belong rather to the province of the professional pastrycook or confectioner than to that of the amateur cook. I have tried, therefore, to give recipes for the sweet course which will be practical possibilities for the amateur cook at home, at the same time using ingredients of Mediterranean cooking, the oranges, lemons, apricots, and almonds, the honey and cream cheese, the eggs, wine, and honey, and, most especially, the fresh fruit of those lands.

A DISH OF POMEGRANATES

Take all the inside from 6 pomegranates and mash them into a silver bowl. Sprinkle with rose-water, lemon juice, and sugar and serve iced.

WATER MELON STUFFED WITH BLACKBERRIES

If by any chance you happen to come upon a water melon and some blackberries in the same season, try this dish.

Cut the water melon in half, take away the black seeds and cut up the red flesh into pieces. Squeeze lemon juice on to it and mix it with some blackberries. Put them back in the halves of melon, add sugar, and put on the ice.

BAKED BANANAS

Peel and split bananas and cut in half. Place in baking dish with butter, brown sugar, orange and lemon juice, nutmeg, cinnamon, a tablespoon of honey, and a glass of rum. Place strips of lemon peel on the top and bake for about 30 minutes in a moderate oven. The sauce should be thick and syrupy.

FRUIT SALAD

Fruit salad can be delicious; it can also be very nasty indeed. Here is a good recipe which includes the making of the syrup which is so important.

2 oranges, 1 apple, 1 pear, 1 grapefuit, 2 bananas, 3 fresh figs, 2 slices pineapple, either fresh or tinned.

For the syrup, bring 2 teacups of water to the boil; throw in 10 lumps of sugar and the peel of an orange cut in strips. Boil for 3 minutes and leave the syrup to cool.

Prepare the fruit carefully, put it into a glass dish and pour over it a small wineglass of maraschino, and the prepared syrup.

It is important that the fruit salad should be very well iced, and it should be prepared several hours before it is needed.

APRICOTINA

¼ lb dried apricots, ¼ lb butter, 2 oz sugar, 4 eggs.

Soak the apricots in water for 2 or 3 hours. Stew them slowly and keep aside 10 or so nice whole apricots for the garnish, and put the rest through a sieve, keeping the juice separately, and reserve 2 tablespoons of the purée, also for the garnish. Now put the purée into a saucepan, and add gradually the sugar, the butter, and the yolks of the eggs, stirring all the time until you have a smooth thick cream. Leave it to cool. Fold in the stiffly beaten whites of the eggs, and pour the whole mixture into a buttered soufflé dish and steam it (on the top of the stove) for 45 minutes. When it has cooled turn the pudding out on to the serving dish. Now spread over the top the purée which you have reserved and on the top of this arrange the whole apricots. For the sauce, mix the apricot juice with an equal quantity of thin cream. This sweet is greatly improved by being made the day before, and kept in the refrigerator, in which case it is preferable not to do the garnishing until an hour before you are going to serve it.

Apricotina is not such a trouble as it sounds; the result should be something between a moist cake and an iced soufflé.

APRICOT SOUFFLÉ

Put ½ lb of cooked dried apricots through a sieve. Put them in a buttered, sugared soufflé dish. Fold in the stiffly beaten whites of 3 or 4 eggs. Bake in a fairly hot oven for 15 to 20 minutes.

COLD ORANGE SOUFFLÉ

1 pint orange juice, about ½ oz gelatine, 2 tablespoons sugar, 2 eggs.

Soak the gelatine in the orange juice for 30 minutes, put the orange juice in a saucepan with the sugar and as soon as it starts to boil take it off the fire and pour gently through a strainer over the well-beaten yolks of eggs. Stir well, and leave to cool. Add the stiffly beaten whites and fold them into the soufflé. Leave in the refrigerator to set, and put whipped cream flavoured with sherry on top before serving.

ESH ES SERAYA *or* PALACE BREAD (an Egyptian sweet)

Heat ½ lb of honey with ¼ lb of sugar and ¼ lb of butter until the mixture thickens. Add 4 oz white breadcrumbs. Cook all together in a saucepan, stirring until it has become a homogeneous mass. Turn out on to a plate or into a tart tin. When cold it will be a soft mass, in consistency not unlike the filling of an English treacle tart, but of course much thicker, and can be cut into triangular portions. This sweet is always served with a cream which is skimmed off the

top of quantities of milk cooked very slowly until a thick skin
forms on the top, so stiff that when separated from the milk it can be
rolled up. A little roll of this cream (it cannot be made from
modern pasteurized milk) is placed on top of each portion of
Palace Bread.

SIPHNIAC HONEY PIE

These quantities fill two 7″ to 8″ shallow pie or flan tins.

 1 lb unsalted *myzíthra* (this is the fresh Greek cheese made from
 sheep's milk; in England ordinary fresh milk or cream cheese can be
 used), 4 oz honey, 3 oz sugar, 8 oz flour, 8 oz butter, 4 eggs,
 cinnamon.

Make a paste of the flour and butter with some water, roll it out
thin and line the tins. Work the cheese and warmed honey together,
add the sugar, the beaten eggs, and a little cinnamon, spread this
mixture on the paste and bake in a medium oven (Regulo 5) for 35
minutes.

Sprinkle the top with a little cinnamon.

BEIGNETS DE PRUNEAUX

Soak prunes in weak tea for 2 hours and then in rum. Stone them.
Make a frying batter* with the addition of a tablespoon of rum and
deep-fry the prunes. When golden, roll them in powdered chocolate
mixed with vanilla sugar.

GÂTEAU DE FIGUES SÈCHES

 1 lb dried figs, 1½ pints milk, 4 tablespoons rice, 3 eggs, 2 oz butter.

In a large thick saucepan warm the milk, put in the rice, let it
simmer very gently for about 15 minutes until the rice is softened
but not cooked through. Leave to cool a little. Gradually add the
beaten eggs, and then mix with the chopped figs and the softened
butter.

Turn the whole mixture into a buttered cake tin or turban mould

* Page 50.

large enough to allow for the swelling of the cake during cooking. A three-pint capacity tin is about right.

Bake in the lower shelf of a very slow oven, gas no. 2, 310 deg. F., for 1½ to 2 hours.

The cake is turned out of the mould, and can be eaten hot or cold.

This is a rather primitive nurseryish kind of dessert, but it is a very cheap one, and owing to the very small proportion of rice to liquid is not stodgy.

Sometimes I add a little grated orange or lemon peel to the milk and rice mixture. I think that dried apricots would be good instead of the figs – and if you like you can spread a thin layer of apricot jam at the bottom of the tin before adding the mixture. The jam gives a decorative appearance when the cake is turned out.

FROMAGE BLANC AUX RAISINS SECS

½ lb of unsalted cream cheese (either home made or the French Isigny or Chambourcy), a few muscatel raisins, a small glass of brandy, sugar, lemon peel, a little cinnamon.

Soak the raisins in water for an hour or two, then simmer them for 10 minutes, adding the brandy (or kirsch), a little piece of lemon peel, and a scrap of cinnamon.

Beat together the cream cheese and 2 or 3 tablespoons of castor sugar, add the raisins and the liquid they have cooked in and if you like a little more liqueur. Put into a muslin and leave in a very cold place to drain for several hours. Serve with a plain biscuit.

FIGUES AU FOUR

In a fireproof dish arrange some slightly under-ripe unpeeled figs. Put in a little water, sprinkle them with sugar and bake them (as for baked apples).

Serve them cold, with cream.

TORRIJAS

The Spanish version of a sweet well known in most European

countries, and designed for using up stale bread. In France it is called *pain perdu*.

First prepare a syrup of ¼ lb of sugar, a coffeecupful of water, a small piece of lemon peel, a pinch of cinnamon, all cooked together for 10 minutes or so. When the syrup has cooled add a small glass of sweet white wine or sherry.

Cut 8 to 10 slices of white bread, about ¼ inch thick. Soak them in milk (about ½ pint), then in beaten egg (1 large egg should be sufficient).

Fry the slices until crisp and golden in very hot olive oil. Pour the cooled syrup over them and serve. Instead of sugar honey can be used to make the syrup.

CENCI

Cenci are good to serve with a cold sweet, mousse, ice-cream, etc.

½ lb flour, 1 oz butter, 1 oz castor sugar, 2 eggs, few drops cognac, pinch of salt, grated lemon peel.

Make a rather stiff paste with all the ingredients. Work it well with the hands and then leave it to rest for a little wrapped in a floured cloth. Take a small piece at a time, and roll out very thin, like paper. Cut into shapes – bows, crescents, plaits, or diamonds, etc. Make an incision in each biscuit with a knife. Dip them into a pan of hot fat, turn immediately and then take them out. When they are cool sprinkle them with castor sugar.

This quantity makes a very large number. Half quantities would be enough for 6 people.

YOGHOURT

Throughout the Balkans and the Middle East yoghourt, or yaourti, is served as a sweet, or as a sauce (as for the pilaff on p. 98), in salad (p. 156); it is eaten for breakfast or at any meal, and is refreshing and light in a hot climate. Try it with brown sugar and hot stewed fruit. Dried apricots are particularly good, fresh damsons, apple purée, blackcurrant purée, quince or bitter orange marmalade.

ORANGE AND ALMOND CAKE

The juice of 2 large or 3 small oranges, grated rind of 1 orange, 4 oz ground almonds, 2 oz fine dry breadcrumbs, 4 oz sugar, 4 eggs, ½ teaspoon salt, cream, and if available 1 tablespoon of orange-flower water.

Mix together the breadcrumbs, orange juice and grated orange rind, add the ground almonds, and the orange-flower water.

Beat the egg yolks with the sugar and salt until almost white. Add to the first mixture. Fold in the stiffly beaten egg whites. Pour the mixture into a 2½″ deep, 2 pint capacity cake tin, buttered and sprinkled with breadcrumbs. Bake in a moderate oven (Regulo 4) for about 40 minutes.

When cold turn the cake out and cover the top with whipped cream (about ¼ pint). Very good and light, and excellent for a sweet at luncheon or dinner.

COFFEE MOUSSE

½ pint milk, 2 eggs, 2 oz sugar, 3 leaves gelatine (rather under ½ oz), 1 after-dinner coffeecupful of very strong, unsweetened black coffee, ¼ pint double cream.

Make a thin custard of the milk and yolks of eggs previously thoroughly whisked with the sugar. Strain and leave to cool.

Put the gelatine leaves cut into small pieces into the prepared coffee in a small pan or a cup, and place this in or over hot water. Stir until the gelatine has dissolved. Leave to cool and strain into the custard.

Whip the cream lightly, amalgamate with the custard. When this mixture is quite cold and just barely beginning to set round the edges fold in the stiffly whisked whites. Turn into a small soufflé dish (¾-pint size) or into small cups or glasses.

Enough for 4.

CHOCOLATE CREAM MOUSSE

To use up 4 egg whites break 2 oz of bitter chocolate into a fireproof dish or bowl. Add 2 tablespoons black coffee, heat 3 or 4 minutes in low oven. Have the egg whites ready whisked into peaks.

Beat chocolate-coffee mixture to a smooth paste, stir in a saltspoonful of powdered cinnamon. Pour the beaten whites on to the chocolate, fold the two together, lifting and turning the mixture. Add ¼ pint lightly whipped cream and a pinch of salt. Turn into glasses or small cups and chill in the refrigerator. Makes 4 or 5 helpings.

CRÈME À L'ORANGE

> 5 oranges, 1 lemon, 4 oz white sugar, the yolks of 4 eggs, a little orange liqueur (cointreau, Grand Marnier or orange curaçao) or sweet dessert wine.

Put the strained juice (there should be approximately a half pint) of the oranges and the lemon together in a saucepan with the well-whisked yolks and the sugar. Heat gently, stirring constantly, as for a sauce or custard. The mixture takes some time to thicken, and is ready when it starts to adhere to the sides of the pan, although it never thickens sufficiently to coat the spoon. Take the pan from the heat and stir the cream until it is cool. By this time it will have thickened perceptibly.

Pour the cream into 4 custard cups or glasses, and leave them overnight in the refrigerator. Do not attempt to turn these creams out or to decorate them with whipped cream. They are intended to be just sufficiently set to be eaten with a spoon and should be accompanied by sponge fingers, soft honey cake, or almond biscuits.

PEARS BAKED IN WINE

A method of making the most intractable of cooking pears very delicious. It is especially suitable for those households where there is a solid-fuel cooker.

Peel the pears, leaving the stalks on. Put them in a tall fireproof pot, or earthenware crock. Add about 3 oz of sugar per pound of pears. Half cover with red table wine, or sweet dessert wine. Fill to the top with water. Bake in a very slow oven for anything between 5 and 7 hours, or even all night, until the pears are quite tender.

These pears, deep rich-red or amber gold by the time they are cooked, are served cold in their remaining juice (it can be thickened to a syrup by a few minutes' fast boiling) with cream or creamed rice separately. For an even more festive and decorative effect the pears can be stuck all over, when cold, with slivers of blanched almonds.

SLICED AND SUGARED ORANGES

One of the charms of restaurants in Italy is the way a waiter will come to your table, spear an orange on the end of a fork, and in a wink it is peeled, and cleanly, elegantly sliced on to your plate, no juice wasted and never a trace of pith or pip. It is an entertaining and skilful professional trick, fascinating to watch, and difficult to imitate. So I prepare my sliced oranges – a sweet dish which I find never fails to please, year in year out whatever the season, by an easier method.

Using a very sharp knife, preferably saw-edged:

(1) Halve the orange horizontally, then divide each half into 4 sections.

(2) Flick out pips, slice off any pith on the outer edge of the section.

(3) Slice the pulp cleanly from the skin straight into a bowl, leaving behind every trace of pith (you have to be a bit wasteful to make these sliced oranges successfully).

(4) Sprinkle the prepared oranges with white sugar, and finally serve them, chilled, in deep wine glasses. According to size of the oranges, allow 1, 1½, or 2 per person, and, if you like, pour a table-spoon of kirsch or cointreau into each glass just before the meal, or perhaps a little lemon juice and a sprinkling of freshly chopped mint leaves; or for a change, and at seasons when oranges are not at their best, pour ordinary red table wine or a little dessert wine such as Cyprus Commanderia over the oranges.

QUINCE AND ORANGE SALAD

Mix sliced oranges with a few quarters of stewed sliced quinces (see recipe on p. 171) and serve in wine goblets.

PEACHES IN WINE

Yellow-fleshed Italian or French peaches are best for this dish.

Allow a minimum of one large peach per person. If the fruit is at all hard or unripe immerse them for a minute or so in boiling water. Extract one at a time and remove the skin. Slice the fruit, preferably into clear glass goblets, one for each person, or, if you are making the dish for a large party, into a deepish fruit bowl or old-fashioned glass or porcelain compote dish on a pedestal stand. Strew the sliced peaches with a liberal amount of castor sugar and lemon juice. Then, as short a time as possible before the peaches are to be eaten, pour over them enough ordinary red table wine to reach just level with the top of the fruit.

A sweetish white wine such as a Monbazillac from south-western France or one of the muscat dessert wines of Provence, Spain, or Italy can be used as an alternative to the red table wine which is more common in French household usage.

FRESH FIGS WITH ORANGE JUICE

Allow two firm, very slightly under-ripe purple or green figs per person. Cut the stalks from the figs but do not peel them. Quarter them, put them in a bowl, and over them pour the juice, freshly squeezed, of one large orange for eight figs. No sugar is necessary, but the fruit should be prepared an hour or so before it is to be eaten.

Presented in a perfectly plain white china salad bowl, or in individual clear glass wine goblets, this fig salad is one of the most beautiful as well as one of the most exquisite of all fresh-fruit dishes.

MELON AND MUSCAT GRAPES

Green-fleshed, yellow-skinned honeydew melons are best for this mixture. Cut the melon in quarters, discard seeds and rind. Slice the flesh into cubes. Put these into a bowl, squeeze lemon juice over them, strew them with sugar. Add a handful of peeled and seeded muscat grapes – or, when they are available, the tiny little white currant grapes imported from Greece or Cyprus, which are eaten skin and all, and need only be stripped from the stalks and washed before they are added to the fruit salad.

QUINCE COMPOTE

Peel, slice, and core 2 lb of ripe quinces. Keep the cores and peel, and with them make a syrup by cooking them in ½ pint of water and 6 to 8 oz of sugar for about 30 minutes.

Strain the syrup, and in it cook the sliced quinces, very slowly, until they are quite soft and can be pierced easily with a skewer.

Serve hot or cold, with thin pouring cream, or with unsalted cream cheese or yoghourt.

Slices of quince prepared as for compote are delicious mixed with sliced, butter-fried dessert apples, and in apple-tarts and pies.

HONEY AND WALNUT CREAM

A Provençal honey recipe.

Pound or chop finely 3 oz walnuts, shelled weight. Mix with them 2 tablespoons of thick aromatic honey (our own heather or clover honey for example) and 2 tablespoons of thick cream.

Spread between thin buttered slices of fresh brown bread, this mixture makes exquisite little sandwiches for tea, or to serve instead of wafers or biscuits with a lemon or apricot ice-cream.

This amount makes about a dozen little sandwiches – but the mixture keeps a long time in a covered jar, so it can be made in larger quantities.

Jams and Preserves

Tarts and Preserves

Corfu: Making the Preserves

****

'Now that the *robola** is safely on the way, the Count can turn his attention to the kitchens with their gleaming copper ware and dungeon-like
ovens. Here he busies himself with Caroline and Mrs Zarian in the
manufacture of *mustalevria* – that delicious Ionian sweet or jelly which is
made by boiling fresh must to half its bulk with semolina and a little
spice. The paste is left to cool on plates and stuck with almonds; and the
whole either eaten fresh or cut up in slices and put away in the great store
cupboard.

'*Sykopita*, Zarian's favourite fig cake, will come later when the autumn
figs are literally bursting open with their own ripeness. But for the time
being there are conserves of all kinds to be made – orange-flower preserve
and morella syrup. While the Count produces for the table a very highly
spiced quince cheese, black and sticky, but very good.'

Prospero's Cell
by Lawrence Durrell

POIRES À L'AIGRE-DOUX

Make a syrup with 1¾ pints of white wine vinegar, 2 lb sugar,
peel of half a lemon, cinnamon. Cook in the syrup 6 to 8 lb of
small peeled pears. Pour into a basin, cover and leave a week.
Strain, put the fruit into bottles, reheat the syrup and pour it
boiling on to the fruit. Cool before covering.

PLUMS À L'AIGRE-DOUX

Ripe but fine plums. Wipe and prick with needle. Make a
syrup as for *poires à l'aigre-doux*, adding cloves and nutmeg
instead of lemon, put them into the boiling syrup. Take each one
out as soon as the skin is lightly broken. Strain them in a sieve, add
the juice to the syrup, reboil it and pour on to the fruit in pots.

* A 'black' wine made in Corfu.

MELON À L'AIGRE-DOUX

Good for serving with a cold chicken or ham.

Peel a 3-lb melon, throw away the seeds, cut in pieces the size of a nut. Blanch 2 minutes in boiling salted water. Strain. Put in cold water, re-strain. Cook 2 minutes in 8 oz boiling vinegar. Put into a basin, keep in a cool place for 48 hours. Strain. Cook the vinegar with 1 lb of sugar and a few cloves. After boiling 15 minutes add the melon. Boil 3 minutes. Pour into a basin. The next day put in pots and cover.

SPANISH QUINCE PASTE

Wash the quinces but do not peel them. Quarter them and remove the seeds. Steam them until quite soft, and put through a sieve or food mill. Weigh the resulting pulp and add the equivalent weight in sugar. Cook in a heavy pan and stir frequently until the paste starts to candy and come away from the sides of the pan.

Turn into square or round tins about ¾ inch deep. Leave to cool. The paste should be left to dry in the sun for several days, but the drying process can be achieved by putting it into a warm oven which has been turned out after the joint has cooked, or into the plate drawer of an electric cooker, or in the cool oven of an Aga cooker. The process need not all be carried out at once, but can be done for an hour or two at a time when it is convenient.

The paste can either be stored in the tins or wrapped in grease-proof paper.

Serve the paste cut into squares, as a dessert, with the coffee.

STUFFED DATES GLACÉ

Remove the stones from 10 oz of dates. Stuff them with the following mixture: 3 oz of ground almonds, mixed with a little hot syrup made with sugar and water. To this add icing sugar until the paste is firm. Stuff the dates with this mixture, and dip in syrup, made as follows:

For the syrup: 7 oz sugar to half a glass of water and a few drops of lemon juice. Cook without stirring, dip a spoon in cold water and then in the syrup, then in water again; if it is covered with a layer like glass, the syrup is ready. With a hatpin take each date and dip in the sugar and with a knife dipped in water put each on an oiled plate. When they are dry put them into little paper cases.

Prunes can be treated in exactly the same way.

PEACH JAM

8 lb peaches, 8 lb sugar, 2 glasses water.

Peel the peaches, break in halves, extract the stones, put the fruit into a preserving pan with the sugar and water. Cook quickly. When the peaches become transparent the jam is done.

PRESERVED MIXED FRUIT

Into good white vinegar pour approximately twice the quantity of sugar making an acid syrup. Leave this for some days. Into it put the fruit,* ripe and dry. At the end of 6 or 7 months, they will be ready. Keep in a cool place in earthenware jars, not too cold or hot.

RAISINÉ DE BOURGOGNE WITH PEARS

Put 4 or 5 lb of ripe grapes through a sieve and reduce the juice obtained by half, taking care it does not stick. Peel some ripe pears, cut in quarters and put them into the juice and reduce another third. The pears will then be cooked.

QUINCE PRESERVE

Peel and cut the quinces (large ones) in four pieces; carefully core and cut out all the hard inside. Now make a note of their weight. Lay them in a saucepan, cover with cold water containing a handful of salt (1½ to 2 oz). Boil quickly till *soft* (for about 10 minutes), then drain quickly. Take the peels and cores and pips, cover with cold water, boil well and strain. Pour this juice into a basin and add an equal quantity of sugar. Pour this mixture over the quinces,

* Plums, peaches, pears, figs, cherries, melon, apricots, etc. To serve with ham, cold turkey, or chicken.

177

arranged in a preserving pan, now add more sugar, equal to the original weight of the prepared quinces. Simmer gently till the pieces are quite clear, and the juice forms a thick syrup when cold.

TO PRESERVE FRESH TOMATOES

Choose ripe tomatoes, medium size, absolutely whole, perfect, and without the slightest crack or bruise. If the tomato has a hole where the stalk is, drop a little wax on it. Roll the tomatoes in a clean cloth and dry well.

Put them carefully into jars with a large mouth, fill the jars with nut oil (*huile d'arachide*) *without taste* so that the tomatoes are covered with a layer of oil an inch deep. On the oil pour a layer of *eau-de-vie* (to prevent the oil from going rancid) half an inch deep. Seal hermetically.

The oil can be used afterwards as it will remain quite tasteless.

STUFFED WALNUTS IN SYRUP

This is one of the traditional recipes of Cyprus kindly obtained for me by Mr Sigmund Pollitzer, of Kyrenia.

> 50 fresh green walnuts, 50 almonds, roasted in their skins, 50 cloves, 6 tumblers of water, 4½ lb of sugar.

Skin the walnuts, as delicately as possible, and put them in a bowl of water; leave them to soak for a week, changing the water every day. Make a small incision in each walnut, into which you put an almond and a clove (the cloves are optional, depending on your taste).

Make a syrup of the sugar and the water, and leave it to cool, then put in the walnuts, bring them to the boil, and simmer for about 20 minutes. Leave them to cool in the syrup, and the next day boil them again for another 20 minutes.

When they are cool put them into preserving jars. They are delicious.

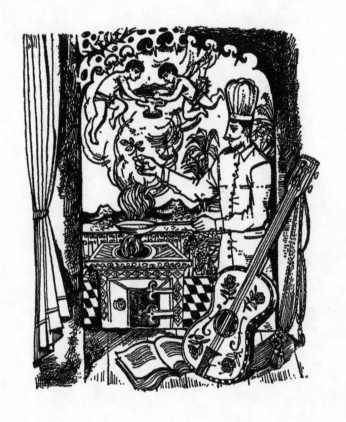

Sauces

The Good Cook

* * * * * * * * * * * * * * * * * * *

'All culinary tasks should be performed with reverential love, don't you think so? To say that a cook must possess the requisite outfit of culinary skill and temperament – that is hardly more than saying that a soldier must appear in uniform. You can have a bad soldier in uniform. The true cook must have not only those externals, but a large dose of general worldly experience. He is the perfect blend, the only perfect blend, of artist and philosopher. He knows his worth: he holds in his palm the happiness of mankind, the welfare of generations yet unborn. . . . If she drinks a little, why, it is all to the good. It shows that she is fully equipped on the other side of her dual nature. It proves that she possesses the prime requisite of the artist; sensitiveness and a capacity for enthusiasm. Indeed, I often doubt whether you will ever derive well-flavoured victuals from the atelier of an individual who honestly despises or fears – it is the same thing – the choicest gift of God.'

South Wind
by Norman Douglas

The first four sauces in this chapter have, strictly speaking, little to do with Mediterranean cooking, but they are classics of the French kitchen, and it is important to know how to make them. Anyone who has mastered the principles of cooking these sauces, and of a mayonnaise, should be able to produce almost any sauce without difficulty, and will be able to improvise to suit themselves.

SAUCE ESPAGNOLE

Sauce *espagnole*, being the basic brown sauce from which many others derive, was usually made in considerable quantity, and kept for several days. This being no longer practical, I give the quantities for making about 1 pint.

> 2 oz bacon or ham, 1½ oz flour, 1½ oz butter, 1 oz carrots, ⅛ gill white wine, ½ oz onion, 1¼ pints good brown stock, thyme, bay leaf, salt and pepper, ½ lb tomatoes.

Melt the bacon or ham cut in dice in a little of the butter; add the carrots, also cut in dice, the onions and the herbs and seasonings; when they turn golden add the white wine and reduce by half.

In another pan put the rest of the butter and when it is melted put in the flour; let it brown very gently, stirring to prevent burning. When it is smooth and brown add half the brown stock, bring to the boil, transfer the mixture from the other pan, and let the whole cook very slowly for 1½ hours. Put the sauce through a fine sieve; return to the saucepan and add the chopped tomatoes and the rest of the stock; let it cook slowly another 30 minutes and strain it again; the sauce should now be of the right consistency, but if it is too thin cook it again until it is sufficiently reduced.

SAUCE BÉCHAMEL

Put 1½ oz of butter into a thick pan; when it has melted stir in 2 tablespoons of flour; let this cook a minute or two, but it must not brown. Add gradually ½ to ¾ pint of hot milk, and stir the sauce until it thickens; season with salt, pepper, and a very small pinch of nutmeg. The sauce should cook very slowly for 15 or 20 minutes, to allow the flour to cook; this precaution is frequently omitted by English cooks, hence the appalling taste of imperfectly dissolved flour. Should the sauce turn lumpy, bring it very quickly to the boil and let it bubble a minute or two; sometimes this eliminates the lumps, but if they still persist pass the sauce through a fine sieve into a clean pan.

SAUCE BÉARNAISE

Even experienced cooks get into a panic when *béarnaise* sauce is mentioned. It is not really so fearsome to make, but it does require the cook's full attention.

Any sauce with eggs in it is best made in a double saucepan, but if there is not one available put a Pyrex or china bowl into a small saucepan half filled with water, and cook the sauce in this; the sauce can be served in the bowl in which it was cooked.

The sauce is made as follows:

In a small saucepan put 2 chopped shallots, a little piece of parsley, tarragon, thyme, a bay leaf, and ground black pepper. Add half a tumbler of white wine, or half white wine and half tarragon vinegar. Let this boil rapidly until it has reduced to 1 tablespoon of liquid. It is this preliminary reduction which gives a Béarnaise sauce its inimitable flavour. Strain what is left of the vinegar into a Pyrex bowl, add a dessertspoon of cold water, and over the saucepan containing hot water, and on an exceedingly gentle fire, proceed to add little by little 4 oz of butter and 4 beaten egg yolks, stirring with great patience until the sauce thickens, and becomes shiny like a mayonnaise. If the fire becomes too hot, if the water in the double saucepan boils, or if you stop stirring for one instant the sauce will curdle; when it has thickened take it off the fire and keep on stirring; the sauce is served tepid, and is at its best with grilled tournedos, but can be used with many other dishes. A very little finely chopped tarragon is stirred in before serving.

If all precautions fail and the sauce curdles, it can sometimes be brought back again by the addition of a few drops of cold water, and vigorous stirring; if this fails put the sauce through a fine sieve, add another yolk of egg and stir again.

The addition of a quarter of its volume of concentrated tomato purée to the *béarnaise* makes sauce *Choron*; 2 tablespoons of meat glaze added to the initial *béarnaise* makes sauce *foyot*. Whatever variations are to be made are made at the end when the sauce has already thickened.

Red wine, although unorthodox, makes just as good a sauce as white wine. Few people realize this.

SAUCE HOLLANDAISE

The same remarks apply here as for sauce *béarnaise* (see preceding page).

Reduce by two-thirds 2 tablespoons of white wine or white wine vinegar, and 4 tablespoons of water, seasoned with a pinch of pepper and salt. Put this reduction into a double saucepan, and add gradually the yolks of 5 eggs and ½ lb of butter; stir until the sauce thickens, adding a spoonful or two of water, which keeps the sauce light. Season with a little more salt, and a few drops of lemon juice; it may be put through a fine sieve but this is not strictly necessary. Sauce *hollandaise* is usually served with asparagus, or with poached sole, salmon, and so on.

For sauce *mousseline* add 4 tablespoons of cream to a sauce *hollandaise*.

SAUCE TOMATE

Chop 2 lb of good ripe tomatoes; put them into a thick pan with salt, pepper, 3 or 4 lumps of sugar, 1 clove of garlic, 1 onion chopped, 2 oz of raw minced beef, and half a teaspoon of sweet basil. Put the lid on the pan and leave the tomatoes to stew very slowly. When they are reduced to pulp and most of the water from the tomatoes is evaporated (this will take 20 to 30 minutes), put the mixture through a sieve. If it is still too liquid put the sauce back into the pan and reduce until it is the right consistency.

SAUCE BOLOGNESE FOR SPAGHETTI

½ small tin Italian tomato paste, 2 oz mushrooms or mushroom stalks, 2 oz minced raw beef, 2 oz chicken livers, 1 onion, 1 clove of garlic, basil, salt and pepper, 2 lumps of sugar, a little oil, butter, or dripping, stock or water, ½ glass wine.

Into a small thick pan put a tablespoon of oil, butter, or dripping. In this fry the chopped onion until it is golden. Add the minced beef, the chopped mushrooms, and the chicken livers. Cook until the beef is slightly fried – only about 3 minutes.

Now add a small glass of wine, red or white, and let it bubble until reduced by half. Put in the tomato paste, add the basil, seasoning and the sugar and enough stock or water to make the sauce of a creamy consistency, but thinner than you finally require, for it will reduce in the cooking.

With the point of a knife crush the clove of garlic and add to the sauce. Put the lid on the pan and simmer very slowly for 30 minutes at least. The longer the better, so that the essence of the meat penetrates the sauce. You can leave it at the bottom of a slow oven for as long as you like. Be sure to have it very hot before serving with your spaghetti.

TOMATO PASTE

The slightly salty, smoky flavour of this sauce in Greek *stiphádo* (p. 81) and macaroni dishes is entirely characteristic; it may not be to everybody's taste but it blends remarkably well with *retsina*, the *vin ordinaire* of Greece, which seems so outlandish when one first arrives there that it is hard to believe that one could ever become accustomed to it. Sooner or later, though, most people do, and sitting in a village *taverna*, the wine barrels stacked around, *retsina* seems the right and proper drink.

Several pounds of tomatoes are chopped up and put in a pan, with a good deal of salt, and cooked until they are reduced to a pulp. They are then put through a sieve, and reduced again over a slow fire. The sauce is then put in bowls and left out in the sun until it has become very dry.

It is stored in jars with a layer of oil on the top to keep out the air.

SAUCE OF DRIED CÈPES* TO SERVE WITH SPAGHETTI

2 to 3 oz of dried cèpes. Cover them with water, add salt and pepper. Simmer for 30 minutes. Strain them, keeping the water they have cooked in, which you strain again through a muslin.

Put this back in the pan, and melt 2 or 3 oz of butter in it.

Serve the sauce and the cèpes over the cooked noodles or spaghetti.

SAUCE CATALANE

This sauce is intended to give the taste of partridge to grilled mutton cutlets.

In a tablespoon of pork fat sauté 1 chopped onion and a little ham cut in dice. Sprinkle with flour, stir with a wooden spoon. Add a glass of water and a glass of white wine, a dozen cloves of

* See note on dried cèpes, p. 123.

garlic and a whole lemon cut in slices. Simmer for 30 minutes. In a mortar pound 6 oz of almonds and stir them into the sauce 5 minutes before serving.

AVGOLÉMONO SAUCE

This is simply the Greek way of making a sauce for practically anything.

The juice of a lemon and 2 or 3 egg yolks are beaten together and added to some of the stock in which fish or meat or chicken has cooked, and stirred carefully until it is thick.

Youvarlakia, or little meat rissoles, served in this sauce are not to be despised, and, as the standby of every Greek cook, how different from the bottled horror and the stickfast of English cooking.

SAUCE CHEVREUIL

2 glasses of red wine (Burgundy if possible), 1½ glasses of stock or meat essence, 2 tablespoons vinegar, 2 level tablespoons sugar, 4 or 5 tablespoons red currant jelly, 2 tablespoons flour, 2 tablespoons butter or lard, half a lemon, a good pinch of pepper.

Put into a saucepan 1½ glasses of the red wine, the vinegar, the sugar and the lemon, peeled and cut into dice. Mix the jelly into this preparation and boil until it is reduced by half. Meanwhile prepare a brown *roux* with the butter and flour, add the stock and the rest of the wine and cook slowly for 20 minutes. Mix the two preparations, put through a fine sieve and reheat.

SAUCE PIQUANTE

In oil, butter, or dripping fry a sliced onion until it is golden, then add a wineglass of vinegar and 2 cups of the stock of whatever meat the sauce is to be served with. Add herbs, a clove of garlic, salt and pepper, and simmer until the sauce is a good consistency.

A few minutes before serving, add a spoonful each of capers and chopped gherkins.

MAYONNAISE

For mayonnaise for 4 people 2 egg yolks are sufficient, and about ⅓ pint of olive oil. I find the best utensils to use are a small but heavy marble mortar which does not slide about the table, a wooden spoon, and for the olive oil a small jug with a spout which allows the oil to come out very slowly.

Break the yolks very carefully into the mortar; add a little salt, pepper, and a teaspoon of mustard in powder. Stir well before adding any oil at all; at first the oil must be stirred in drop by drop, then a little more each time as the mayonnaise gets thicker. Stir steadily but not like a maniac. From time to time add a *very* little tarragon vinegar, and at the end a squeeze of lemon juice. Should the mayonnaise curdle, break another yolk into a clean basin, and add the curdled mayonnaise gradually; it will come back to life miraculously.

SAUCE TARTARE

Sauce *tartare* is a mayonnaise to which you add finely chopped tarragon, capers, parsley, chives, and a very little pickled gherkin and minced shallot.

SAUCE VINAIGRETTE

The basis of sauce *vinaigrette* is olive oil and good wine vinegar; ⅔ oil to ⅓ vinegar, with the addition of a little finely minced onion, parsley, tarragon, capers, chives, chervil, and lemon peel, all stirred together with a seasoning of salt and pepper.

TURKISH SALAD DRESSING

3 oz of shelled walnuts, a breakfastcupful of clear chicken or meat broth, or milk, 4 tablespoonsful of dried breadcrumbs, salt, cayenne pepper, lemon juice, parsley or mint, a clove of garlic.

Pound the walnuts and garlic to a paste; stir in the breadcrumbs, then the broth or milk, season with salt, lemon juice, and cayenne pepper. The sauce should be about the consistency of cream. Very good with salads of haricot beans and chick peas. Enough to season ½ lb of either of these vegetables. Sprinkle the salad with fresh herbs before serving.

AÏLLADE

A mixture of garlic, basil, and grilled tomatoes, pounded in the mortar. Olive oil is added drop by drop, until thick.

MOHAMMED'S SAUCE FOR FISH

Mayonnaise, 2 hard-boiled eggs, 3 anchovies (boned and chopped or 4 anchovy fillets), 2 teaspoons of capers, 2 level tablespoons of finely chopped celery, 2 tablespoons of peeled, chopped fresh cucumber, a little grated onion or shallot.

Stir all the chopped ingredients into a cupful of stiff mayonnaise, then add the grated raw onion or shallot to taste.

AÏOLI

Aïoli is really a mayonnaise made with garlic, and sometimes breadcrumbs are added.

It is served usually with salt cod, or with boiled beef, accompanied by boiled carrots, potatoes boiled in their skins, artichokes, French beans, hard-boiled eggs, and sometimes with snails which have been cooked in water with onions and fennel, or with baby octopus plainly boiled, with pimentos; in fact, with any variety of vegetables, but always cooked *à l'eau*. It is one of the most famous and best of all Provençal dishes. The *aïoli* sauce is itself often called *beurre de Provence*.

Start by pounding 2 or 3 cloves of garlic, then put in the yolks of eggs, seasonings, and add olive oil drop by drop, proceeding exactly as for mayonnaise. Add lemon juice instead of vinegar.

SKORDALIÁ (the Greek version of *aïoli*)

2 egg yolks, 2 oz ground almonds, 2 oz fresh white breadcrumbs, ½ dozen cloves of garlic, ¼ pint olive oil, lemon juice, parsley.

Pound the garlic in a mortar, then add the yolks, the olive oil drop by drop as for mayonnaise, and when of the right consistency stir in the ground almonds and the breadcrumbs. Add plenty of lemon juice and chopped parsley. This sauce curdles very easily; if it does, start again with another egg yolk as for mayonnaise (p. 187).

Some versions of this sauce are made without egg yolks. A more primitive and an easier system.

SAUCE À LA CRÈME D'OURSINS

In Provence, *oursins* (sea urchins), as well as being eaten as an hors d'œuvre, are made into a most delicate sauce. The coral is scooped out of 2 or 3 dozen *oursins* and pressed through a fine muslin. There should be about 2 oz of purée, which is then incorporated either into a sauce *mousseline* or a mayonnaise, and eaten with plainly cooked fish, or with cold lobster.

TAPÉNADE

Tapénade is a Provençal sauce. The name comes from the word *tapéna*, Provençal for capers. It is a simple sauce and excellent for hard-boiled eggs, cold fish, or a salad of cold boiled beef.

Pound 2 tablespoons of capers in a mortar with half a dozen fillets of anchovies; add olive oil little by little as for mayonnaise, until you have about a cup of sauce. Add the juice of a lemon and a little black pepper, but no salt, as the anchovies will probably be salty.

SAUCE ROUILLE (a Provençal sauce for fish)

1 clove of garlic, 1 red pimento, breadcrumbs, olive oil.

Grill the pimento whole until the skin turns black. Take out the seeds, rub off the burnt skin, rinse the pimento in cold water, and pound it with the garlic. Soak a handful of breadcrumbs in water and squeeze them dry. Add them to the pimento and then stir in very slowly 4 tablespoons of olive oil. Thin the sauce with a few teaspoons of the stock from the fish with which it is to be served.

SYRIAN SAUCE FOR FISH

A teacupful of fresh white breadcrumbs, 2 oz of pine nuts or walnuts, the juice of a lemon, salt.

Soak the breadcrumbs in water, then squeeze dry. Pound the pine nuts or walnuts to a paste. Mix them with the breadcrumbs, add salt and the lemon juice. Press through a coarse sieve. Serve poured over a cold baked fish. If too thick add a few drops of cold water or broth from the fish.

CAPPON MAGRO SAUCE

A large bunch of parsley, a clove of garlic, a tablespoon of capers, 2 anchovy fillets, the yolks of 2 hard-boiled eggs, 6 green olives, fennel (either a bunch of the leaves or a slice of the fleshy root-stem), a handful of breadcrumbs, a large cupful of olive oil, a little vinegar.

Remove the thick stalks from the parsley, wash the leaves, put them into a mortar with a little salt and the clove of garlic. Pound until it is beginning to turn to a paste (this is not so arduous a task as might be supposed). Then add the capers, the anchovies, the stoned olives, and the fennel. Continue pounding, and add the breadcrumbs, which should have been softened in a little milk or water and pressed dry. By this time there should be a thick sauce. Pound in the yolks of the hard-boiled eggs. Now start to add the olive oil, slowly, stirring vigorously with a wooden spoon as if making mayonnaise, and when the sauce is the consistency of a thick cream add about 2 tablespoonsful of vinegar.

This is the sauce which is poured over *cappon magro*, the celebrated Genoese fish salad made of about twenty different ingredients and built up into a splendid baroque edifice. The sauce is an excellent one for any coarse white fish, for cold meat, or for hard-boiled eggs.

TOMATO SAUCE WITH PEPPERS *or* PEBRONATA

A Corsican sauce used in conjunction with braised or stewed beef or gigot of kid. I have also had it, in Corsica, with thick slices of fried country-cured ham.

Ingredients are:

> 1 small and 1 large onion, 1 large or 2 small cloves of garlic, a tablespoon of chopped parsley, a branch of dried thyme or a half teaspoon of dried or fresh thyme leaves, 1 lb of very ripe tomatoes, 4 tablespoons of olive oil, 6 very small green peppers or 2 or 3 larger ones, a glass (4 to 6 oz) of rough red wine, a heaped teaspoon of flour, salt, a half-dozen juniper berries.

Chop the small onion together with the parsley and garlic. Heat two tablespoons of the olive oil in a shallow pan. Put in the onion and garlic mixture. Add the thyme. After five minutes' gentle cooking put in the tomatoes, unskinned but roughly chopped. Season with salt. Add the crushed juniper berries. Simmer steadily for about 15 to 20 minutes.

Meanwhile peel and slice the large onion. Put it in another pan with the remaining 2 tablespoons of olive oil, warmed.

Let it melt very gently. When the onion is yellow and soft add the green peppers, washed, all seeds and core discarded, and sliced into, roughly, one-inch lengths. When the peppers are slightly softened, stir in the flour. Then add the red wine, heated in a separate saucepan. Stir well, let the wine reduce by two-thirds.

Now press the tomato sauce through a fine wire sieve into a bowl. Pour the resulting purée into the pepper and wine mixture. Cook gently for another 5 minutes or so. The peppers should not be too soft.

Pebronata sauce is strongly flavoured, dark, aromatic, and interesting, with a character rather different from that of any other Mediterranean sauce.

For a beef stew to which this sauce is added see the recipe for *pebronata de bœuf*, p. 83. White wine is specified for the initial cooking of the beef. If it is more convenient, more of the same red wine used for the sauce can go into the beef stew.

Index

****

Aïgroissade toulonnaise, 131
aïoli, 188
  in bourride, 64
Aleppo chicken, 109
almond and orange cake, 167
ambelopoùlia, 150
anchovies
  in anchoïade, 40
  in anchoïade Croze, 41
anguilla in tiella al piselli, 62
apricots
  apricotina, 162
  soufflé, 163
arní souvlákia, 77
arroz a la catalana, 97
artichokes and broad beans, 133
artichokes, Jerusalem, soup, 19
aspic jelly, 141
aubergines
  à l'arménienne, 130
  beignets, 129, 130
  dolmas, 130
  in fritters, 129, 130
  in marinade, 151
  in mousaká, 37
  in ratatouille, 131
  salad of, 151
avgolémono sauce, 186
  soup, 17

bananas, baked, 162
basil, whole, dried, 64
Basque soup, 17
batter, frying, 50
beans
  broad
    with artichokes, 133
    with bacon, 133
    brown, Egyptian (fool), 105

beans – *contd*
  haricot
    aïgroissade toulonnaise, 131
    cassoulet toulousain, 102
    fasoúlia, 137
    rissoles of beans (ta'amia), 137
    salad, 155
    soup, 19
    ta'amia, 137
becfigues. *See* Figpeckers
Beckford, William: 'Alcobaca', 109;
    'Portuguese Supper Party', 93
BEEF
  culotte de bœuf au four, 83
  en daube à la niçoise, 82
  filet de bœuf
    à l'amiral, 83
    flambé à l'avignonnaise, 83
    à l'italienne, 81
  langue de bœuf en paupiettes, 38
  à la mode à la provençale, 146
  pebronata de bœuf (Corsican
    ragoût), 83
  stiphádo (Greek ragoût), 81
beetroots
  to bake, 26
  soup, iced, 26
beignets
  aubergines, 129
  courgettes, 129
  pruneaux, 164
  sardines, 62
Bennett, Arnold, 'A Greek
    Restaurant', 73
blackberries in water melon, 161
boar, saddle of, Norman Douglas's
    recipe, 88
bocconcini, 74
bœuf. *See* Beef

193

INDEX

INDEX

INDEX

OTHER NEW YORK REVIEW CLASSICS*

For a complete list of titles, visit www.nyrb.com or write to:
Catalog Requests, NYRB, 435 Hudson Street, New York, NY 10014